HOW TO MAKE SENSE OF THE WORLD AND YOURSELF

Life

Talal Alali

Published by Liberty In Print

First edition

ISBN 9781739308636

To Anna

Contents

Preface   9

Chapter 1.
Introduction   14

Meeting the real victims   14
'You don't know how to live'   22

Chapter 2.
How psychology helps you   28

Psychotherapy   30
Who is normal?   32
The 4 Ds: danger, distress, dysfunction and deviance   35
Mental health and trauma   38
'I want to keep living'   40
Psychiatric medications   44

Chapter 3.
Cases from psychotherapy   55

Limits of psychotherapy   56
'I'm not the same since I lost my dad'   58
'My older brother lost his mind'   63
'I am fine – I just need a little help'   66

Chapter 4.
Irrational beliefs and their cost   71

Having kids is a burden and living alone is beautiful   71

The gay gynaecologist   74

Loneliness is hell   77

Victimization   80

A wrong diagnosis   82

'We are all sick and need help'   86

Mass delusion: from Epicurus to current activists   90

Marxism is the cure   92

There is no reality   96

Chapter 5.
Self-help books between science and opium   100

The superpower within you   100

Immune to truth   105

Why do they reject the facts?   108

Who are you?   110

It's a secret   113

Unlock your potential   115

Stop wasting your money on cafés   123

Self-change is easy   126

The world is a small village   130

Chapter 6.
Understand yourself   133

The 'self' in psychology   133

Key questions for self-reflection   135

Chapter 7.
Understanding others   142

How can I change her (him)?   142

Cluster A: the eccentric   144

Cluster B: never-ending war   145

Cluster C: the anxious shadows   147

Cluster B in detail: the elephant in the room   148

Questions for relationship evaluation   153

Chapter 8.
The real solution   155

A life-long journey   156

Preface

Do psychologists understand the world better than others? Can they give advice regarding marriage, relationships, money, friendships or parenting? Do they know how to live their own lives well?

'You learn more from real experiences than from books', 'I'm not sure I've applied my academic knowledge to my daily life', and 'There's a difference between science and individual experiences' are common responses, unfortunately.

A prominent psychologist specializing in child psychology was once asked if his specialty made him a good father. This was his reply: 'I'm not that sure what I know was any use when it came to raising my children. You know, the cobbler goes without shoes.'

Many academics I have met over the years seem to separate what they do from how they live their lives. Another prominent professor told me he regretted studying psychology since it is not appreciated by the general public, is tainted with white-washing, and made him miserable.

In contrast, I have known many psychologists who are extremely proud of their specialty. They would say, for example: 'Psychology is the summit of sciences; it aims to understand humans and improve their condition. Consider how many people have benefited from psychotherapy, IQ tests, from various psychological services. Look how it examines complex issues such as memory and the nervous system. Numerous researchers have studied the impact of childhood traumas, showing they may have long-lasting effects on us. Other studies, which showed that the differences between females and males are not categorical, have contributed to improving the quality of human lives. Without the insight of psychology, life would have been considerably worse off.'

A brilliant psychology professor in City College of the City University of New York (CCUNY), once told me that people study psychology or psychiatry either due to their own psychological issues or to help someone they care about. Typically, individuals drawn to psychology are keen on understanding themselves in a profound and honest way.

Before I invite readers to explore this book, I would like to reflect on how deeply psychology has impacted my own life and why it may matter to you.

Growing up in a middle-class family with two working parents during tumultuous times in Kuwait, I was affected both directly and indirectly by various conflicts in the Middle East, including the Iraq–Iran war, the Arab–Israeli conflict and the Lebanese crisis. As I navigated my childhood, Kuwait, like much of the Middle East, was undergoing an intense identity transformation. Events such as the Islamic revolution in Iran, the siege of Mecca by radical Islamists, and the rise of extremist Islamic factions had significant psychological and social impact not only on the people living in my homeland or in the wider Middle East but also much further away.

This era was marked by a stark conflict between the push for modernity and the pull of deep-rooted tradition, fracturing the social fabric into fragments of confusion and resistance. People were torn between their desires for modern personal freedoms, human rights, democratic traditions and a collective culture and tradition that controlled every aspect of life. Many radicals and traditionalists wanted to impose their way of life on everyone, while reformists demonstrated remarkable resilience.

Many people around me grappled with psychological disorders, and their condition was as evident as their fear of being labelled crazy in a stern society.

When I was 12, I witnessed how my best friend's sister began to suffer from mild seizures. Her parents panicked: in our traditional culture, a girl must be healthy to marry and have a family, and there was a strong stigma against mental disorders. Hoping it would pass, they initially chose to ignore her condition. What puzzled me was how everyone acted as if there were nothing wrong with her.

However, as her seizures persisted, her parents turned to a well-known Islamic preacher who claimed he could treat all kinds of diseases. He lived lavishly, with a huge house and several wives, supported entirely by the fees charged for reciting religious texts over desperate patients, many of whom were from supposedly educated families.

The girl was taken to him twice, and sometimes three, times a week, with each visit incurring a hefty fee. During these sessions, the preacher would recite holy texts in a loud voice over her, which only made her seizures worse and further degraded her mental and social abilities. Gradually, she became a shadow of her former self. She started stuttering and her cognitive abilities began to decline.

As her condition deteriorated, her parents sought another well-known and more expensive preacher who employed cauterization alongside recitation. He burned her several times to 'release the demon'. Fortunately, two of her teachers intervened and managed to get her referred through the school's clinic to a hospital, where doctors diagnosed her with epilepsy. Despite this professional diagnosis, it took months before her parents allowed her to start the prescribed medication.

Although she seemed to outgrow that experience, completing her studies, securing a good job and becoming fully functioning, she never recovered fully from the trauma inflicted by her parents and the charlatans who exploited her suffering for profit. She confided in me a few years ago that the abuses she endured continue to affect and spoil her life, leaving deep scars that have not yet healed. Witnessing her ordeal and similar cases during my childhood had a great impact on me, sparking a deep curiosity about human nature. When I enrolled at Kuwait University, I initially intended to study science. However, my passion led me to explore various subjects, ultimately graduating *cum laude* in psychology. After working for a few years, I pursued further studies in the United States on an academic scholarship from Kuwait University. I studied English at Western Michigan University before earning my MA from City College of the City University of New York. Subsequently, I enrolled at Manchester University for my PhD and finally settled at Edinburgh University, where I earned my doctorate.

Studying psychology in three different countries has greatly benefited me. I was lucky to meet many authentic thinkers and researchers who enormously affected me – not only through their extensive knowledge but, most importantly, through their decency and integrity. As a student at City College of New York City, Columbia University, John Jay College of Criminal Justice, Manchester University, the University of Edinburgh and Kuwait University, I was privileged to be learning from such exemplary figures. They were successful, committed to the scientific method, genuinely compassionate and dedicated to making the world a better place.

Chapter 1.
Introduction

MEETING THE REAL VICTIMS

'They are fools and crooks, every single one of them. They don't deserve what they have. These idiots are swimming in money, living like kings. Someone needed to teach them a lesson, and I'm happy if I was that person. Trust me, they enjoyed what was happening. Don't believe them when they complain and whine. I didn't force anyone to do anything. How could I? If anything, I helped them. I didn't hurt anyone.'

This was one of Sami's honest replies when I asked if he regretted defrauding the investors in his companies. Over time, he gave me many answers. Sometimes he denied doing anything wrong; other times, he bragged about it.

Conversations with Sami are brain-poisoning for me. He is a habitual liar who consistently insults his audience's intelligence. He uses his body language and words to intimidate and control his audience. Over the years, he has succeeded in deceiving people, making them believe his words rather than their own eyes. In fact, many of his victims still believe his lies, even though he has been indicted by the courts. He has warned investors against filing complaints against him, promising to repay all the money to those who do not sue him. The extracts below come from interviews with Sami, an inpatient in a forensic psychiatric ward.

'What about your ex-wife Sara? Do you feel any remorse for what you did to her?' I once asked him.

'Absolutely not. She was nothing but a spoiled idiot. When she met me, she was nothing. I made her. Her pretentious father and silly mother treated her like a princess. Can you imagine? That ugly, fat imbecile thought of herself as a princess, and someone actually believed it. No decent man wanted her. She went out with every scumbag in the city. She would never have gone out with me if a man from her circle had wanted her. She was so happy I showed interest in her. She and her family are racists, but they accepted me because they knew that I was way better than them and, actually, my people are better than theirs. Now she's playing the victim. She cheated on me, not once or twice, and because I'm kind and noble, I forgave her. I shouldn't have done that. She was begging me not to divorce her.'

'You took millions from her. You abused her physically countless times. I've seen her medical reports. You even implicated her in criminal activities without her knowledge.'

'If she didn't know, then she deserves to be punished. If she didn't enjoy being beaten, why did she stay with me? Why would she stay with a monster? If she had any self-respect, she would have left.'

'So, it's not true that you kept apologizing to her, promising to change, and even threatened to kill yourself if she left you?'

I had seen the court records containing WhatsApp messages between the man and his wife, in which she showed him her wounds and medical reports, and he recorded

15

voice messages crying and begging for forgiveness and asking her not to go to the police.

'Either she's an idiot for believing me and forgiving me, or these incidents happened a few times and I didn't mean them. She was the main cause. I'm human. If someone keeps hurting you, taking advantage of you, disrespecting you, lying to you, it's natural to snap. If it were another guy, he would've killed her.'

'What about taking her money?' I asked.

'Money? What money? I didn't take anything from her or anyone else. And even if I did, it would be much less than what I deserve. I wasted my life with that fat idiot. I should get a Nobel Prize for enduring her stupidity. It wasn't her money, anyway. Her father and grandfather built their wealth by exploiting the poor. It's only fair we take it back. They're the true criminals. I came from poverty and misery. I've suffered throughout my life because of people like Sara and her family: my whole life has been a trauma. Everyone is quick to blame me, but no one considers the causes.

'I'm the true victim here. I was assaulted by my own father, who pretended to be kind and respectable while he was hurting his own children – the very person who was supposed to protect us. He used to beat me for no reason. I was so terrified of him that my heart would palpitate whenever I heard his voice or smelled the cologne he wore. Can you believe that my mother has never hugged me? She detests me. She never wanted me. She only cared about herself, her makeup, her many guys, but never her children. Now she's after my money. My childhood was an endless nightmare. Night after night, I was beaten to suppress my cries, but the tears wouldn't stop – I was hungry, lonely and scared. Nobody cared about me. It's not fair. I've been suffering all my life while these rich people enjoyed theirs.'

Attempting to steer the conversation to a different subject, I asked, 'Do you love your children?'

'Of course I do. I'm the best father in the world. It's tragic that my children are just as wicked as their mother; they refuse to see me.'

At the time of the interview, Sami had not seen his children in three years.

When I decided to become a psychologist, I was what you could describe as a warrior for justice, albeit a naive one. I was influenced by a socialist understanding of history and humanity, constantly sought novelty and hoped to impress laypeople. I detested the rich and successful, believing they exploited the poor, and was convinced criminals were victims of society. I argued that punishment was the problem, not the solution, and that the death penalty was cruel and ineffective. I believed that the entire concept of punishment and reward was obsolete and that levelling the playing field and making all groups equal could create a just, progressive society. Convinced that if we stopped locking up drug addicts and decriminalized drug use, we could solve the addiction crisis, I thought that helping addicts was far more effective that jailing these victims of society.

Somehow, despite listening to these ideas countless times, a nagging doubt never went away. After I got my PhD, I did not want to be an armchair researcher. When I was teaching students and answering their questions, I would sometimes feel I did not have scientific evidence for what

I was teaching. Yes, these ideas came from a textbook and were confirmed by correlational studies but I realized these were not conclusive evidence. I discovered that a PhD in psychology only starts you on the long journey towards understanding complex human nature. This qualification prepares you to educate yourself if and only if you are willing to take a stand and test your ideas. Working in mental health institutions, where you deal directly with patients, psychiatrists and the law is crucial to gaining the insights needed to understand the vast amount of dense psychological and psychiatric literature. You discover that textbooks sometimes lie and many prestigious journal articles are misleading.

Dealing with individuals diagnosed with personality disorders in general and antisocial personality disorder and psychopathy in particular has been one of the most eye-opening experiences for me. I believe it is vital for every human to understand personality disorders and how to deal with those who have them. As psychologists, our mandate when dealing with patients, including psychopaths, was to extend compassion and treat them in a professional manner without judgement, even when making an evaluation. We were told to listen attentively to their fabrications and demonstrate empathy, as per professional guidelines. This allows us to understand these pervasive disorders in a more comprehensive way. It allows us to understand how these people reason, feel and interact.

Among the early patients I saw, Sami stood out as a particularly interesting character. He was diagnosed with both psychopathy and antisocial personality disorder and deemed to be dangerous to others. To my surprise, Sami had a striking similarity with many people I knew in private life. I am not sure if any of them were ever diagnosed, but they seemed to reason and behave like Sami. Like him, they hurt others but never sincerely regretted it. Some might have broken the law but were never caught, while others made sure they were not breaking any laws but still caused significant pain to vulnerable people.

Initially, Sami tried to charm and convince me he was a kind person victimized by society through no fault of his own. He frequently spoke of his miserable childhood, his altruistic nature, of the many people he had helped over the years and how they had backstabbed him. He never failed to remind me of his once-powerful status, assuring me he would soon return to the limelight. Over time, he realized I saw him as nothing more than a charlatan. I did not believe he could justify his crimes by blaming others. To me, he was the prototype of a psychopath who lies as naturally as he breathes and takes pleasure in hurting others. He had made a fortune and held a high office for many years, not in spite of, but because he was a psychopath. His heyday ended abruptly when his corrupt boss was ousted from power, and Sami was charged with embezzlement, money laundering and organized criminal activity. Sentenced to 10 years in prison, he was transferred to the psychiatric ward due to his connections.

I studied him, among others, thoroughly – a practice we psychologists are not usually encouraged to undertake. I met with his parents, relatives, some of his victims and friends. I reviewed his school transcripts, medical records and criminal records. I watched recordings of media interviews from when he was wealthy and powerful and scrutinized his social media accounts. I spent countless hours talking with him, trying to uncover what his mask of sanity concealed. He agreed to participate in a longitudinal study a colleague and I were conducting, completing numerous scales and questionnaires. After many months, my colleague and I confirmed the forensic psychiatrist's conclusion.

Yes, Sami came from a troubled home, but he grossly exaggerated the abuse he had endured, often to stir up guilt and attract sympathy from listeners – a tactic he used to take advantage of people. He had never been raped, nor had he grown up in poverty. In fact, he was not very different from his mother, except that he deceived more people than she did.

She told me in our first meeting how every man in her life had taken advantage of her, including her father. She also expressed constant thoughts of ending her life to escape her lifelong suffering. However, her affect and body language were inconsistent with the exaggerated emotional language she used. She was flirtatious and cunning. Sami's father, one of her several husbands – or victims – married her for her money and his lack of self-esteem. Her relationships with her children were complex and troubling. Her older daughter refuses to speak to her, describing her mother as manipulative and resentful of others' happiness. All the people I interviewed concurred that Sami was most like his mother, who, in turn, seemed to both favour and despise him simultaneously.

The fact is, I found Sami fascinating in a way. If you read The Mask of Sanity by Hervey Cleckley and live with Sami or interact with him the way I did, you realize how accurate Cleckley's description of psychopaths is.

Sami did his utmost to show everyone that he was well connected, had travelled the world and knew many girls. He always threw in fancy words, scientific concepts and the names of important people to dazzle his listeners. The glimpse – or superficial charm – he projects is a double-edged sword; over time, many people grow tired of it and realize that it's all a fabrication. He constantly seeks to impress strangers, particularly those in positions of power. He jumps from one topic to another just to promote himself. He lies for the sake of lying. He enjoys making promises he doesn't intend to keep.

Sometimes, he resembles a fiction writer, making up stories to captivate his audience. The only difference is that their goal is to harm his hearers rather than entertain them. Another difference is that he is the main character of his plot and the story is almost always the same: you watch him save the day when everyone else has failed, or he is the victim of societal injustices, or the intelligent, benevolent hero of myriad adventures. He will tell you how he travelled the world, did scuba diving and skydiving, studied law and has a keen interest in psychology. One consistent observation I have made over the years is that psychopaths display an intense interest in understanding and controlling others.

The impulsivity exhibited by psychopaths is of a different calibre from that of normal individuals. While the latter can be impulsive, it comes with limits and, in most cases, does not result in harm to other people.

Over the years, I have conducted numerous interviews with individuals diagnosed with antisocial personality disorder and psychopathy. I recorded and transcribed many of these interviews with the permission of the interviewees, intending to use them for research. However, I now find it more valuable to share them in this book rather than in technical papers. The following extracts are taken from an interview with an inpatient in a forensic ward.

'YOU DON'T KNOW HOW TO LIVE'

'I wish I were a doctor: I would've travelled the world and had a different girl every night. You don't know how to live.'

This is what Ahmad said as we were finishing our second interview. He then asked me if he could be frank, and when I agreed, he continued.

'You know, I married over sixteen girls. Once, I married two girls in less than a month, and it did not cost me a penny. I met a Malaysian girl on a dating site. They are so kind and trusting. I told her that I was an important person and that I was working two jobs to help my family. She was madly in love with me even before we met in person. She paid for my ticket and when I arrived, I proposed, and she said yes. We had a small wedding, and she paid for everything. She was caring and beautiful but very boring as well. You know, after a week, I was so bored with her. She did not speak Arabic, and my English is not that good. We decided to spend our honeymoon in Malaysia, and then she would quit her job and prepare to move to Kuwait with me. She was busy dealing with all kinds of things in the morning, and I would kill time by going to malls.

'One day, I saw another girl; she was working in a quaint little shop not very far from the hotel where I was staying with my wife. Again, I couldn't resist. I fell for her. It took me a week to convince her to marry me. Her parents did not approve, but she loved me so much that we registered the marriage, and I took her on a honeymoon to Indonesia. I took all my stuff from the hotel when my wife was out and left with my new wife.

'In Indonesia, we had a great time. But, you know, I couldn't bring her home. She thought I was rich and single, while I was married, had a kid, and was living at my mum's house. So, I did the same: one day I just ran away and forgot about them. From time to time, I look at our pictures and regret not keeping those girls.'

Ahmad was charged with attempted murder after he pushed one of his wives in front of a speeding bus. She sustained severe injuries but, somehow, survived. She and the bus driver testified against him, and the police uncovered incriminating evidence, including a life insurance policy he had purchased a few months before the incident and text messages to his brother where he mentioned plans to get rid of his wife. Despite this, Ahmad kept denying any wrongdoing, claiming his wife jumped in front of the bus while he tried to stop her. He was sent to a mental institution for evaluation, which concluded that he was responsible for his actions and diagnosed him with antisocial personality disorder, concluding that he posed a danger to others.

Another man told me how he once reported his nephew to the police. He wanted to convince me he was a decent person, hoping I would support his request to be released from the mental institution. Despite being indicted multiple times for selling drugs, he did not like drug dealers, he said. Although he admitted to taking drugs on and off for many years, he did not sell unless in need, he affirmed. His nephew, on the other hand, was an evil person, making a fortune selling drugs to children and taking advantage of girls. Believing his nephew deserved to be behind bars, he cooperated with the police to ensure justice was served. To protect himself, he convinced his nephew that another guy was the snitch, not him.

I asked him whether he was the one who introduced his nephew to drugs. He replied that his nephew was a grown-up man who made his own choices. If he did not want to be an addict, he should have said no.

Sami's wife told me that when she first met him, she thought she had hit the jackpot. He was charming, soft-spoken and modest. He told her he was changing careers: although he had studied law and wanted to be an academic, he decided to become a pilot since he loved travelling and could not stay in one country for long. He also mentioned owning several businesses and drove an expensive sports car. She said she was impressed by how nice and kind and gentle he was. At that time, she was in a toxic relationship with someone who didn't give her much attention, wasn't committed or loyal to her, and was uncertain about starting a family. Then Sami came along and proposed to her on their second date. She thought this was a bit awkward but, at the same time, he seemed like a decent, direct and straightforward person. He puzzled her with stories of his childhood suffering, the fact that he came from a minority, and how people often looked down on him and his people for no reason. He portrayed himself as an independent, intelligent man with several university degrees. She said the whole thing felt like a dream – or a nightmare. Not even a month passed from the day she met him to the day she found herself married to him.

Months later, she had their first child. During the first six months, he was still nice and kind, but she began uncovering his lies. He said he did not have any uncles or aunts, yet she discovered he had five. He said he had two university degrees but, in reality, he had dropped out in the first semester. The various cars he drove turned out to be rented. He had a minor job, possibly in a government department, when they were dating. It was with her money and influence that he obtained a law degree from a poor Arab country where paying the fees guaranteed a qualification.

After obtaining that degree, his wife arranged for him to appear on television giving legal advice, and he became widely known. Unfortunately, he got involved in various schemes. He ran for election and lost by a small margin but was soon recruited by some big guns and became part of a network within the establishment. They used him for several tasks. On their behalf, he carried out illegal activities, including money laundering, and, in the process, became very wealthy and attained high positions. Everyone believed he was rich, which he was, but it was his wife's money that had got him there. Her father was impressed with him because he always knew what to say. He would bend over backwards to please his wealthy, powerful father-in-law, and used the latter's companies for his own benefit.

Sami began cheating on his wife or, to be more accurate, he never really stopped. She kept discovering incriminating phone calls, messages, emails, pictures of other women, deleted conversations and phone calls from strange numbers. Initially, she believed his explanations, but as more people reported seeing him at various places, her suspicions grew. Each confrontation ended with his passionate denials and indignant outrage. 'How could you think that of me?' he would shout, justifying himself and turning the tables on her, accusing her of being paranoid, selfish, a bad mother, a bad wife, spying on and disrespecting him.

Despite everything, she wanted to stay with him. She thought her life was settled: she was married, had three kids and her husband was a well-known, successful lawyer. She justified the situation to herself thinking that no one can have everything in life.

Unfortunately, or perhaps fortunately, Sami had a different plan. He was involved with another woman, who was far richer and more connected than his wife. The only complication was that she was married, and he believed she would leave her husband for him. However, she had a different agenda – seeking fun, lavish gifts and temporary diversion.

After he took out numerous loans and sold work permits and visas through his wife's company, he divorced his wife, expecting to start a new life with his affluent lover. But the other woman told him she had changed her mind – she had discovered she still wanted to be with her husband.

Sami did not change – he changed us.

He spent two years in the psychiatric ward attending talk therapy sessions, meeting with counsellors and social workers. He claimed to be depressed and requested prescriptions for medication, which he received but would rarely take. He kept trying to brainwash and take advantage of people. Eventually, he was isolated from the other patients, was transferred back to jail and spent another two or three years there before being granted an early release.

In just a few months, he launched new businesses and reappeared in magazines and newspapers.

In a phone call a few years later, a colleague sarcastically told me, 'We are the fools. I saw Sami last night – he was driving a beautiful car with a stunning young woman sitting next to him.'

Chapter 2.
How psychology helps you

Attempting to understand the human psyche – including feelings, thoughts and behaviours at both individual and societal levels – is an ancient endeavour that has evolved through various stages. The great Greek philosophers sought to comprehend human nature, to distinguish between and describe the different groups of people, to explain thought processes, predict behaviours and suggest ways to improve human lives.

Understanding, and thus being able to predict and control human behaviour, as well as providing convincing answers to pressing questions about life, death, feelings and interactions are among the most powerful tools for gaining power, wealth, fame and success.

During the Dark Ages, religious institutions and authorities controlled what are now thought to be the main questions in the field of psychology. These institutions often provided superstitious answers designed to be upheld rather than critically investigated. Many questions were not addressed. For centuries, psychological enquiries were censored. Dissatisfied intellectuals and ordinary people tried to understand themselves and others through simple observations and introspection. The conclusions of these observations often contradicted the authorities' explanations. In many societies around the world, people with mental disorders were often considered as possessed by evil spirits. Exorcisms were, and in many societies still are, a source of income, power and fame for individuals and institutions.

The authorities heavily regulated and enforced how people could live their lives and satisfy their libido as well as other biological needs. Ways to improve mental health, quality of life and cognitive abilities were entrusted to those who claimed to have perfect answers, yet without giving objective evidence for their claims.

The scientific study of psychology began in the latter half of the nineteenth century when German researchers started using experimental methods to examine the physiological aspects of behaviour. Since the early twentieth century, psychology has branched into many different schools, each specializing in specific aspects of behaviour or adopting distinct research methods. Significant discoveries have been made in understanding human behaviour, cognition and mental health.

Prominent figures in the development of psychology as a scientific discipline included Wilhelm Wundt, often regarded as the father of experimental psychology. Wundt made history when he established the first psychology laboratory at the University of Leipzig in 1879, marking the formal beginning of psychology as an experimental and scientific discipline. His work laid the foundation for future research in psychology.

Another key figure is Sigmund Freud, a neurologist who revolutionised the field by founding psychoanalysis, a method for treating mental illness through dialogue between a patient and a psychoanalyst. Freud's theories on the unconscious mind, the development of sexuality, and the mechanisms of repression profoundly shaped both psychology and Western culture.

Behaviourism, led by figures such as John B. Watson and B.F. Skinner, emerged as a dominant school of thought in the early twentieth century. It focuses on observable behaviours and the ways they can be conditioned through reinforcement and punishment.

Cognitive psychology, which gained prominence in the mid-twentieth century, focuses on the study of mental processes such as perception, memory, reasoning and problem-solving.

PSYCHOTHERAPY

Psychology emerged from dissatisfaction with the medical model, which focused mainly on chemical imbalances and biological factors in treating mental disorders. Pioneers such as Sigmund Freud, Carl Jung and Aaron Beck, emphasizing the complexities of the human mind, sought to address the limitations of this approach by developing psychotherapy.

Freud, a neurologist and psychiatrist, observed that many patients showed symptoms of neurological disorders without any biological basis. He noticed that when patients were allowed to speak freely, they revealed unconscious conflicts and struggles stemming from childhood experiences. Freud developed psychoanalysis to explore these hidden processes through techniques such as free association and dream analysis. He believed that understanding and resolving these deep-seated issues could lead to deeper, lasting healing than through medication alone.

Carl Jung, at first a close associate of Freud, expanded on these ideas with his analytical psychology. Jung, also a medical doctor, worked in psychiatric hospitals, where he encountered patients with severe mental illnesses resulting from societal influences and early experiences. He introduced concepts such as the collective unconscious and archetypes, emphasizing the shared, universal aspects of human experience. Jung believed that psychological problems were opportunities for personal growth and transformation, facilitated more effectively through psychotherapy rather than medication.

Aaron Beck, the founder of cognitive behavioural therapy, shifted the focus from unconscious processes to conscious thought patterns. Beck, a psychiatrist, argued that addressing these problematic thinking patterns was more effective in treating mental disorders, especially mood disorders, than when focusing solely on childhood experiences. Cognitive therapy involves identifying and challenging cognitive distortions – those annoying, faulty thought patterns that spiral into negative emotions and behaviours.

Other pioneers of psychotherapy include Alfred Adler, Carl Rogers and Viktor Frankl. Adler, a physician, developed individual psychology, emphasizing social connections and feelings of inferiority as driving forces in human behaviour. Rogers, also a medical doctor and founder of person-centred therapy, stressed the importance of a supportive therapeutic environment that allows individuals to explore and understand their feelings, leading to personal growth. Frankl, a neurologist and psychiatrist, brought us logotherapy, which emphasizes the search for meaning in life as the central human motivational force.

These figures recognized that understanding the root causes of mental distress and aiding personal growth and insight were crucial for lasting change. While medications can play an important role, they do not offer the comprehensive, personalised treatment talk therapy can provide. Through their various therapeutic approaches, these medical doctors underscored the need for a comprehensive view on mental health, one that goes beyond managing symptoms.

Thomas Szasz, who wrote the famous book The Myth of Mental Illness, argued that deviation is not a mental illness. He maintained that individuals with psychological problems need understanding, support and to learn personal responsibility, rather than medication.

Despite all the advances in psychiatry and psychology, understanding and diagnosing mental disorders remain a challenge.

WHO IS NORMAL?

In the fields of psychiatry and psychopathology (mental illness), human behaviour is categorized into three main areas: cognition, affect and executive functions. *Cognition* encompasses all types of information processing, *affect* includes feelings and emotions, and *executive functions* relate to all kinds of expressions of behaviour. Mental disorders typically impact the three functional domains at once, often disrupting an individual's ability to think, feel and act in adaptive ways. Unfortunately, many people – including psychiatrists and clinical psychologists – tend to overlook or seem unaware of this three-part theoretical foundation.

It is important to note that these three areas are interconnected: emotions influence and are influenced by thinking and executive functions. Before a diagnosis can be made, the mental disorders must have been affecting all three domains over significant periods of time.

Cognition

Cognition refers to the mental processes involved in gaining knowledge and comprehension, including thinking, knowing, remembering, judging and problem-solving. Cognitive impairments in mental disorders often manifest as distorted thinking patterns, irrational beliefs, ruminating about traumatic or severe past experiences, and persistent negative thoughts. These cognitive distortions are notably prevalent in mood disorders such as depression, anxiety and obsessive-compulsive behaviour, where individuals may exhibit patterns of irrational, harmful and distressing thinking that cannot be refuted with logic and evidence. All-or-nothing thinking, overgeneralization and catastrophizing are among the common distorted thinking patterns.

Emotions

Emotional instability, characterized by the inability to manage the intensity and duration of emotional responses, is a key element of many mental disorders. It is particularly evident in conditions such as bipolar disorder and borderline personality disorder, where emotional swings are unpredictable and extreme. Mood disorders disrupt a person's ability to create and maintain appropriate feelings and emotions.

A person with generalized anxiety disorder cannot stop intrusive feelings of worry and fear. The intense fear that paralyses the person's life is overpowering and is beyond his or her control. Similarly, a person with borderline personality disorder cannot stop the pervasive fear of abandonment.

A depressed person sees the world through a lens of gloom and sadness, regardless of external circumstances. This means their emotional state remains unchanged even if something good or bad happens to them or their loved ones. Their persistent sadness is disconnected from actual events, highlighting the serious nature of their emotional dysregulation.

Executive functions

Executive function involves a wide range of behaviours, from basic activities such as sleeping to working to harmful actions such as violence towards others, self-injury and suicide. Depression impairs people's ability to carry out daily chores. Those with antisocial personality disorder tend to engage in reckless behaviours, including reckless driving, gambling, drug use, promiscuity and violence. Patients with borderline personality disorders exhibit impulsive behaviours and are prone to engaging in self-harm and maintaining multiple relationships.

The interplay between cognition, emotions and executive function is crucial for understanding mental disorders. Effective treatments need to address all three components to achieve optimal outcomes.

THE 4 Ds: DANGER, DISTRESS, DYSFUNCTION AND DEVIANCE

Danger (in reference to cognition, executive function and feelings), distress, dysfunction and deviance are the four crucial markers used to differentiate between people who are healthy and those with mental disorders.

How do you know if you are suffering from psychological disorders rather than just being sad or angry? Negative emotions are essential for our functioning. We need fear, anger, sorrow and regret to lead a normal life. Feeling sad or angry does not lead to your being depressed in the clinical sense.

The cause of being depressed is: unsolved conflicts, according to psychoanalytic theory; destructive ways of thinking, according to the cognitive theory; maladaptive learning experiences, according to behavioural theory. Hence, depression is not the same as normal emotions that last a long time or become overwhelming.

Many people think depression is sadness. However, this is far from the truth. Sadness, anger and all the other so-called negative feelings are adaptive and helpful, vital for preserving human life and maintaining a good quality of life. When we fail a test, feeling sad and upset with ourselves is what motivates us to study and fix our mistakes. When we realise someone has been taking advantage of us, indignation and anger are what make us stand up for ourselves to prevent more damage.

To the contrary, people who suffer from clinical depression may not feel sad when they fail an exam or feel indignation when discovering their partner has been unfaithful to them. They are unable to experience adequate positive or negative emotions. They constantly have a low mood, low self-esteem and loss of interest or pleasure and are preoccupied with self-loathing, guilt, helplessness and hopelessness.

'Some people are just a little depressed, so they are not sick. Others have a moderate amount of depression and are hence on the verge of illness. Once you reach a specific level of depression, you need medication' – this is one of the fallacies many people still believe. But the reality is that mental illness is clearly defined; it is a categorical construct: people are either sick or not sick. Of course, after being diagnosed, there is a spectrum of severity of the disorder.

Danger

Driving in Beirut or Kuwait is dangerous. It was not always like this, but has been for many years now. Several factors contribute to this situation. Among these are the poor condition of the roads, lax traffic laws and the fact that people drive while under the influence. All that said, locals can still easily distinguish between a reckless, dangerous driver and 'the usual' dangerous driving, such as, for instance, driving slightly over the speed limit. Danger involves behaviours and mental states that pose a risk of harm to the individual or others. This includes suicidal tendencies, aggressive actions or self-harm.

This idea of danger is used in certain mental health diagnoses, where risky behaviours are important indicators of a person's state of mind. For instance, the way in which people with borderline personality disorder or manic depression (bipolar disease) engage others in romantic relationships is dangerous to the person being engaged. One of the main markers for a diagnosis is whether individuals pose danger to themselves or others. Sane people love themselves and love life. Harming oneself indicates that the person is behaving in a pathological way.

Distress

Distress refers to significant psychological suffering and discomfort experienced by an individual over a considerable period of time. This involves negative feelings that are pervasive and chronic.

In depression, people often describe feeling dead from within, noting symptoms such as 'My mouth is bitter and dry, I don't enjoy anything and nothing saddens me. I feel such pain and life is colourless for me.' Psychiatrists use both subjective and objective methods to establish distress, including self-report of the individual as well as observing their affect and voice tone.

Dysfunction

Dysfunction involves a disruption in the ability to perform necessary daily activities and fulfil responsibilities, affecting areas such as work, school or personal relationships. This criterion focuses on the inability of people with psychological disorders to perform essential functions such as working, studying or maintaining personal relationships.

Deviance

Deviance includes behaviours that diverge from expected norms, such as hearing voices no one else can hear or odd beliefs such as being spied on by aliens. It is important to consider cultural perspective within these criteria, though this is not without controversy and has its limitations. For example, in many Middle Eastern cultures, belief in invisible creatures called jinn is common and not seen as deviant. However, if someone claims to be in contact with jinn, they may be considered for admission to an institution, even without their consent.

MENTAL HEALTH AND TRAUMA

It is estimated that around 70 per cent of people experience at least one traumatic incident in their lives. According to some reports, up to 1 billion children aged 2–17 have experienced physical, sexual or emotional violence or neglect. People in countries that have witnessed wars are particularly vulnerable to trauma due to the collapse of institutions and the nature of wars. How individuals react to the traumatic experiences related to warfare are a profound example that can shed light on the human psyche. Many scientists approach mental disorders as natural consequences of trauma.

In 2006, while collecting data for my PhD thesis in Iraq and Lebanon, I expected to encounter helpless people seeking aid and waiting for sympathy. My main hypothesis was that people exposed to trauma would develop a pathological reaction and serious cognitive problems. Based on the literature, I believed there was a positive correlation between the severity of the trauma and the likelihood of pathological reaction.

I met many devastated people who seemed to have lost the will to live, the vast majority of whom had not suffered personally. I also met many people who used the chaos and disorder to harm others. Militias composed of criminals and illiterates were setting up checkpoints, killing people based on their identity and looting their belongings. Individuals formed gangs to loot public property and sell it on the black market. I saw people looting the furniture of an old public school, carrying away old worn-out chairs and blackboards with a weird joy. Gangs specialising in rape were common in some areas as well.

But I also met many remarkable people who were getting on with their lives, fulfilling their obligations and making a positive impact on their society, despite their personal suffering. Nurses, bakers, academics, policemen and rubbish collectors carried on with their duties despite the dangers and uncertainty. They worked amid suicide bombings, terrorism and sectarian wars, unsure if they would get paid. I witnessed countless couples walking by the river or sitting in neglected parks holding hands as if there were no war or bombing. I was impressed by taxi drivers fighting over customers, willing to take the risk to provide for themselves and keep life going. The way restaurant workers strived to please their customers and to see hardworking medical staff filled my heart with joy. Many of these individuals deserve to be role models. Understanding how they managed to remain psychologically intact and carry on with their duties is something from which we need to draw lessons.

In psychology, our focus often lies on individuals with disorders rather than the ones who managed to retain their mental health. In the context of war and other similar adverse experiences, we focus on the negative impact on people's psyche. However, the results of most studies show clearly that the vast majority of people do not develop lasting psychological disorders in reaction to adverse experiences. Despite this, we rarely focus on how and why most people survive traumas, maintain their mental well-being and lead fulfilling lives.

'I WANT TO KEEP LIVING'

During 2005 and 2006, I spent time in Iraq at the height of the civil war and insurgency. The country was engulfed in bloody carnage, with suicide bombings, assassinations, random attacks, and senseless killings becoming commonplace. My research focused on understanding how and why people could survive such severe traumas.

A colleague suggested I include in my study Huda, a woman who had lost her two children in a recent suicide attack. We visited the modest restaurant where she worked, and after that I conducted several interviews with her, which I recorded with her permission. During our conversations, I found her to be very ordinary in some respects and very special in others. Although she was 52, she appeared much younger. Sometimes she spoke in a confident voice, and at other times with shyness. She was very assertive yet calm while discussing her childhood.

She was 18 when she got married, but her husband had died young, leaving her with three boys. Her eldest son married at the age of 20 and had two gorgeous daughters, she told me. Less than two years before I met her, two of her sons were killed in a suicide bombing. They were at a café where a foreigner blew himself up, killing and injuring dozens. She showed me pictures of her sons and the two granddaughters. She explained that for a long time during her marriage she had been dependent on her husband and his salary, but after he died, the money she received was not enough. So, she began doing small jobs here and there, mainly working as a tailor from home, to support her children. She was relieved when they started working but she continued her small jobs.

Huda said she had suffered a nervous breakdown after the deaths of her two sons. However, two or three weeks after the breakdown, she started seeing the world in a completely different light and made a decision.

'I don't want to die, and being sad is very selfish. Staying at home crying and waiting for other people to give me food and care for me and my kids was painful. I felt disgusted with myself. I remember one day I was outraged when I saw an evil neighbour giving my granddaughter a toy and some sweets – he had a disgusting smile that hurt me. I realized I had let everyone down – my granddaughters, my children, my husband. I had let myself down. Why was I allowing this? There was nothing wrong with me. I wasn't disabled: I could do what anyone else could do.'

A few weeks after her children's death, Huda decided to rely on herself.

'I went out searching for a shop to rent. People thought I was mad. I had lost my mind and should see a doctor. Actually, I did go to a doctor. She gave me some medication, telling me to use it if I needed to. I took it once or twice. It wasn't effective. Also, I didn't want to get used to medication. I thought of myself as fine and thought there was no time to waste, and I didn't want to let my loved ones down. I didn't know much about business, but was confident I could learn. I know how to cook and deal with people, so I decided to open a café selling coffee and light food. I decided to open it far away from where I lived. I started searching different parts of the city. I wanted a new, clean place in a nice but not overly rich area. I was so happy when I found this beautiful shop! I loved it because I could see many people passing by it. Over time, I turned cooking and serving my customers into my art. I know how to cook – I've been cooking all my life. And if I didn't know how to make something, I could learn.

'I asked people who had businesses for advice and they told me I would most likely go bust. They also told me I needed a budget for at least six months ahead. I sold whatever gold I had, paid six months' rent up front and bought all the supplies I needed. I didn't hesitate. Even if I lost all this money, it wasn't that important. I didn't care that much. I thought I would sell something else I had. If I've sold all that gold and nothing works, I'll sell the TV. In fact, I did sell the TV to buy nice chairs for the café, and other stuff too. I don't care; I've never cared.

'Some people wanted to help but I didn't take anything from anyone – not my brother, not my sister, no one. I didn't want anyone to claim they'd helped me.

'People told me it would take several months before the business started making money, but it wasn't even two months and I was already making good money. Customers kept coming to my shop, and I felt happy and proud with myself. I bought the most expensive bikes for my grandkids and beautiful jewellery and clothes for their mother. She's such a kind, beautiful lady – hopefully she will get married soon: I've been encouraging her. Many people said I was crazy as I should keep her to help me. But she's like my daughter, and I want her to have a good man in her life and her own business so she won't depend on anyone.

'I do cry and feel sad and miss my kids. I feel that what happened shouldn't have happened and I'm deeply saddened that these beautiful children didn't get to live their lives. On the other hand, I know that every morning I need to put on my apron, prepare my goods and go to my shop. I know I need to support these beautiful kids, and I know I still have a wonderful son who helps me, who's kind and who's living his life. I also want to live what is left of my life to the fullest. I'll die one day, but until then I should live. I'm not a sad victim, I'm not miserable, and I hate it when people look at me with pity. I don't want anyone to pity me. In fact, I'm stronger and better than most people who live fake lives. I'm living a great life, surrounded by people I love.

'I can tell you something else: at this age, I'm in love. I found someone I really like who cares about me deeply and treats me with kindness. I'm taking it slow, savouring the small things in this life, and many things cheer me up and fill my heart with joy. When I get something for my son, my granddaughters or even the man I like, it makes me incredibly happy. I enjoy having breakfast at my place, and I feel so good knowing that I'm independent and can take care of myself.'

In my research, I found that people construct themselves, others and their experiences in a complex, multifaceted way, which usually includes contradictions. During an interaction, we tend to present a specific version or angle 43

that is designed to achieve particular ends within that interaction. For example, exaggerating mental problems and even presenting him- or herself as insane is beneficial for an individual undergoing a forensic evaluation to establish if he or she is fit to stand trial for killing a partner. In contrast, a wealthy person who does not want to be placed under the guardianship of her children may attempt to exaggerate her cognitive abilities.

PSYCHIATRIC MEDICATIONS

Medications are not a one-size-fits-all solution for psychological problems. Psychological disorders are not caused by a sudden chemical imbalance in the brain, and thus, they cannot be 'fixed' simply by taking psychoactive chemicals. How can a pill heal a traumatic experience, overwhelming fear, or an intrusive idea?

Drugs often do more harm than good. Every psychoactive drug has side effects. Who wants to gain weight, lose libido, suffer from nausea, and so on just to deal with depression? These arguments, and many more, are common worldwide. Even some psychiatrists oppose psychiatric medications, arguing that the side effects outweigh their benefits.

Although the above views are widespread, and not without merits, they tend to overlook the reality faced by those suffering the pain of serious mental illness. The person in the fire has a different viewpoint from someone looking on from an armchair. Someone suffering from mental illness is in an incredibly painful, paralysing state. It can be

overwhelming, making the psychological pain almost too

much to bear. For centuries, people have sought the cause of mental disorders and ways to heal them. In many cases, controlling the symptoms of certain mental illnesses can mean the difference between life and death.

The reality of psychiatric medications

Contrary to the belief that psychiatrists prescribe medications needlessly, most psychiatrists do not enjoy prescribing them unless they think they will help the patient. People generally seek psychiatric help because they are in serious distress, not because they want drugs. While a minority may misuse mental health services, the majority seek help out of genuine need. Moreover, while some psychiatrists may harm their patients unintentionally or for personal gain, most are compassionate, ethical professionals dedicated to helping their patients.

Still, overprescription and misdiagnosis are serious problems. Some psychiatrists may prescribe medications too quickly – sometimes before completing a thorough evaluation. This can lead to inappropriate treatment and worsen the patient's condition. A 2011 study in *Psychiatric Services* found that approximately 25 per cent of patients who received psychiatric medications did not have a formal diagnosis supporting such treatment. This highlights the need, first, for thorough assessment and, second, careful prescribing.

Many problems in psychiatric treatment stem from patients' lack of awareness about the diagnostic process. Some patients tend to exaggerate their pain and symptoms, while others downplay or hide their suffering. This is found not only in mental health clinics but is common across the board in medicine. However, it is more dangerous in mental health due to the reliance on what the patient *says* about his or her problem rather than relying on, say, the facts delivered by a blood test or an X-ray.

Patients often tailor their self-reports based on how they want to be seen. For example, some may feel that admitting to sleeping well and having no issues with eating could lead to their anxieties not being taken seriously. On the other hand, some may avoid admitting they struggle to sleep or function well, fearing they will be seen as a hopeless case and hence dismissed by the therapist.

Cultural influences also play a role in how people speak about their medical conditions. The ways people express and report their pain can vary greatly across cultures. This phenomenon has been observed in various studies, especially of Mediterranean patients (such as in Italy) and German patients. Mediterranean cultures typically view pain as something major that needs attention. Therefore, people from these cultures may be more vocal about their discomfort, using dramatic language and gestures to convey the severity of their pain. In contrast, German patients tend to downplay their pain. This approach is influenced by cultural values that emphasise self-control and endurance. Germans tend to keep complaints to the minimum and avoid drawing attention to their suffering.

What is more, many patients are not entirely sure about their daily activities and symptoms, making it tough for therapists to get an accurate picture of a condition. As a result, therapists need to approach the diagnostic process sensitively and carefully, often cross-checking patient statements with other sources of information, such as statements from family members or previous medical records. This is crucial for developing an accurate diagnosis and effective treatment plan.

How effective are psychiatric drugs?

Psychotropic medications (drugs that affect the way a person thinks, feels or behaves) are more effective for some mental disorders than others. For example, when it comes to post-traumatic stress disorder (PTSD), the US Federal Drug Administration has approved two medications: sertraline (Zoloft) and paroxetine (Paxil). The efficacy of these drugs in treating PTSD has been supported by various studies. For example, research published in 2000 in the *Journal of Clinical Psychiatry* demonstrated that both sertraline and paroxetine, compared to a placebo (a substance or treatment with no therapeutic value, such as a sugar pill), greatly reduced PTSD symptoms.

However, like all medications, these drugs come with side effects. Common side effects of sertraline and paroxetine include nausea, dizziness, drowsiness, dry mouth, loss of appetite, increased sweating and sexual dysfunction. These side effects can vary in severity and may affect patients' willingness to continue taking the drug.

Many psychiatrists also prescribe other drugs, from either the same class as sertraline and paroxetine or different classes, which they find effective. This practice often relies on a trial-and-error approach, especially with dosage adjustments. The medical philosophy behind this practice is grounded on the need to alter the patient's mental state to reduce his or her psychological pain and control symptoms, thereby allowing the patient to rest and carry on with the normal activities of life.

The trial-and-error approach is common because individual responses to psychotropic drugs can vary widely. For example, a study in the *Journal of the American Medical Association* found that while selective serotonin reuptake inhibitors (SSRIs) are generally effective, individual response rates can vary greatly, with about 30 to 40 per cent of patients losing their symptoms, and others feeling a partial effect or none at all. Due to this variation, personalised treatment plans must be put in place and the patient must be closely monitored by healthcare providers to maximise his or her healing and minimise side effects.

Furthermore, the use of drugs in psychiatry often involves off-label prescribing. This means that doctors may prescribe medications for conditions other than those for which they were originally approved. This practice is based on clinical experience and growing evidence suggesting that certain medications can help a wide range of symptoms and disorders.

While the trial-and-error method and off-label prescribing can be controversial, they reflect the complicated, individualised nature of psychiatric treatment. Each patient's unique neurobiology (nervous system and how chemicals affect it), psychological history and response to treatment need a flexible approach. This ensures patients get the best care possible, tailored to their own needs and circumstances.

In summary, psychotropic drugs are vital in the treatment of many mental health disorders. Their use, especially in complex conditions such as PTSD, involves a careful balance between their effectiveness and control of their side effects. The practice of trial-and-error in finding the right drug and dosage, along with off-label prescribing, highlights the need for personalised treatment in psychiatry. Such care aims to reduce psychological pain and control symptoms, ultimately helping patients reach a better quality of life.

Drugs and addiction: the paradox

Every year, approximately 3.2 million people die due to alcohol and drug use. Countries as different and far apart as Afghanistan, Yemen, Iran, Colombia, Mexico, and Peru are devastated due to drugs.

The relationship between drugs and humans is both complex and ancient. Historical accounts from Mesopotamia, ancient Egypt, the Roman Empire, and ancient Greece reveal three primary categories of drug use: medical, religious, and recreational. Physicians and pharmacists from thousands of years ago experimented with various substances, documenting the beneficial uses of opium and alcohol as anaesthetics during operations. In non-medical contexts, societies have long differentiated between acceptable and unacceptable substances. Alcoholic beverages such as beer and wine were widely consumed and socially accepted, while opium and cannabis were less common and less accepted.

The regulation and control of drugs have evolved over time, reflecting shifts in understanding of their negative consequences. The Code of Hammurabi includes rules that regulate the distribution and consumption of beer in taverns. Throughout the ages, societies have resorted to banning drugs and punishing addicts, producers, and dealers after witnessing the detrimental effects of drugs on individuals, families, society, and the state. Drug addiction can reach a point where addicts represent a serious threat to the society in which they live. Addiction becomes a burden on the economy as it makes people unproductive and more likely to become involved in crimes. Countries worldwide are forced to divert resources from education, science, innovation, and the care of vulnerable people, such as children, the elderly, and the disabled.

Societies vary in the way they deal with drugs and addiction, oscillating between strict prohibition, severe punishment, and decriminalisation. Neither solution is perfect, and both contain injustices. Those who argue for a middle-of-the-road approach in dealing with drugs often offer nothing but empty rhetoric. Ultimately, the question is, should society consider addiction a crime and restrain addicts, or should we think of them as suffering from an illness, allow them to continue using drugs, and provide financial aid and clean needles for injecting themselves?

Many politicians have risen to power, and writers have gained fame and money, by claiming that we cannot end addiction through punishment and restraint. Such politicians urge people to vote for them and buy into the theory that addicts are victims, not criminals, and need help, not punishment. They argue that society should accept and help addicts overcome their ailment. Some even claim that criminalising drug use is the problem. If all drugs were legal, they argue, we would have fewer problems. People would lose interest in drug use and we would save the money spent on jailing drug dealers and addicts. Others take a middle ground, suggesting we should criminalise drug production and dealing but not drug use, and allow

some drugs but not others.

Notes from a rehab centre

Working in rehab centres, and not the many books and papers I have read, has changed my perspective. On my first day at a rehab centre, after I had received my PhD and joined a university, I gathered the recovered inpatients, who expected a lecture. Instead, I sincerely wanted to listen to them, not talk. I told them I did not officially work at the centre and hence had no authority there. I was there to listen, if they wanted to talk, and those who did not want to be there could leave and I would sign that they had attended. Those who did not want to talk did not have to, but I appreciated it if those willing to talk would be candid. There would be zero consequences, and I did not know anyone personally. Also, the workers were sitting in the front row, so they could not see who was talking, and I asked them not to look at the speakers. The head of the centre nodded in agreement, but it was obvious he was concerned.

I asked who wanted to use drugs right then. Many raised their hands. These were supposedly recovered addicts who had detoxed and completed a course of psychotherapy and were ready to go back to halfway houses or the streets. One of them who raised his hand said, 'Should we lie? We are all here because we want drugs, and if we were not forced, we would never have stopped.' When I asked how their drug addiction started, and if they were willing to explain the effects of the drug on them, several volunteered to discuss their personal experiences.

One said he did not like drugs or enjoy being under the influence, but all his friends were drug addicts. They introduced him to drugs and turned him from being an ambitious university student into a loser and criminal rejected by his own family. Now he had no one but these friends who did nothing but use drugs and then find ways to buy more.

Another told me he discovered in therapy that he was a neglected child and had never loved himself. He did not think he was good or smart, and drugs made him happy and alleviated his low self-esteem.

Yet another told me I was asking the wrong question, as people should be free to use drugs if they wanted to: 'This is my body, and if I want to ruin it, it is up to me. If society wants to help us, they should provide us with drugs or money to buy drugs, but they don't. This is why we steal and prostitute to pay for our needs.'

One common theme among their replies was that they admitted to having committed crimes to finance their addiction or while being intoxicated. They knew the harmful effects of drugs on themselves and society. When they heard a person who had never used drugs telling them drugs are dangerous, they laughed inside because they saw him or her as naive.

'He doesn't think that we have brains and know that drugs are harming us. We experience pain non-stop. We suffer financially. We have left our children, destroyed our families and been in jail. Most importantly, an addict is constantly humiliated and degraded by the dealers, the police and society.'

A guy interrupted him to say he had caused several horrific car accidents because he drove while under the influence. In the last accident, his friend who was sitting next to him died, and another passenger in the other car also died. He spent a year in hospital. 'After all that, someone would come to tell me that I need to quit drugs because they are harmful!'

One girl said that she would never ever take drugs again. She had been clean for over two years and was there of her own free will. She was going into a crisis and wanted to stay in the rehab centre so she would not use drugs again. She then discussed the humiliation and abuse she had endured due to her addiction.

'The cruelty and sickness of the drug dealers, other addicts and even some of the police and practitioners were unimaginable... There are no words that can describe what they did to me... They took away my humanity and treated me in a way that is beyond degrading... A pimp who was my boyfriend enjoyed torturing me, making me act like a dog on a leash... I hated myself but couldn't stop.'

She was introduced to drugs by an ex-boyfriend before she was 20 years old. She was from a wealthy and powerful family. Her father wanted her to stop taking hard drugs; he did not mind what he saw as less harmful drugs. But she did not listen to him. Her addiction worsened with time. At first it was something she enjoyed, then it became a painful part of her life and, eventually, it *became* her life.

She became obsessed with using, and the minute she took drugs and felt the euphoria that usually lasted only a few seconds, she would start worrying about the next dose. For many years, she and her friends were sheltered from the police. She had enough money to cover her use and more. Her father took her to the rehab centre several times and never gave up, but she was not ready to quit. She went through several abusive relationships, mostly with other addicts. Her family kept supporting her despite the damage she continued to cause them. Things changed when her brother discovered she had introduced his daughters to drugs. He was furious when he found out his 15- and 16-year-old daughters were taking drugs – he didn't want them to end up like his sister. Her father also could no longer protect her. He reported her and her drug dealers to the police and her journey with jails, rehab centres and halfway houses started. She told me that despite her countless relapses, she credited the prisons and mental health institutions with keeping her alive: 'I would have overdosed and died if not for jail.'

I have met countless people who have struggled with addiction and were sheltered from the law for a long time. They did not fear the police or courts, and had secret access to drugs. But this did not make them less harmful to themselves or others. Many told me that what they regretted the most was that they had ruined the lives of young people.

Chapter 3.
Cases from psychotherapy

Unexpressed emotions will never die. They are buried alive and will come forth later in uglier ways.

Freud, *Studies on Hysteria* (1895),
co-authored with Josef Breuer

In order to understand how people see themselves and evaluate their experiences, they must be allowed to express themselves freely, to speak without being judged or interrupted, directed or corrected. Afterwards, it is crucial to consider what they have said over an extended period of time rather than relying on isolated statements. It is also essential to compare subjective evaluations with objective indicators and put the data within perspective. It is not enough to take what a person has said during one interview and consider it a representation of who that person is. This applies to psychotherapy as much as it applies to our social interactions.

To judge the effectiveness of psychotherapy, we need to understand its limits and rely not only on objective but also subjective indicators. Psychotherapy should always be held accountable within scientific standards.

LIMITS OF PSYCHOTHERAPY

In his seminal book *The Boy Who Was Raised as a Dog*, Bruce Perry describes the case of his first child patient, Tina. Her story highlights the limits of psychotherapy, the complexity of human nature and effects of society. Tina, a 7-year-old girl, was referred to Perry's clinic because she was aggressive and behaved inappropriately towards her classmates. It was discovered she had suffered two years of rape and violence at the hands of a 16-year-old boy who was the son of her babysitter. Tina did not know her father and had been left by her mother in the care of a neighbour, the boy's mother.

Perry recounts that in their first session Tina, who was 7 years old at the time, wanted to perform a sexual act on him. His explanation was that she had never had a caring male figure:

> She had only known men as sexual predators: no loving father, no supportive grandfather, no kind uncle or protective older brother had touched her life. The adult males she'd met were her mother's often inappropriate boyfriends and her own abuser. (Chapter 1, p. 2.)

Then he details how he worked with Tina for three years. He highlights how he saw her progressing and becoming a normal child. She became calm and stopped performing sexual acts.

To his disappointment, Tina was caught performing fellatio on an older boy at school. Perry explains the girl did not overcome her trauma and did not change; in other words, she did not abstain from engaging in sexual acts – she simply learned how to hide them. He attributes her abnormal behaviour to the rape and sexual abuse she suffered for two years starting when she was just 4 years old.

One can argue that the explanations do not directly derive from the facts or capture the whole picture. Tina was a neglected child living with her mother, who was a single, poor, uneducated woman incapable of looking after herself, let alone raising two children. If we say that Tina did not have a caring male, did she have a caring female figure?

The fact that the rape and abuse of a young child lasted for two years without the mother or neighbour noticing is a clear indication that Tina was neglected. She was a victim of an immoral father, an abused and immoral mother, and a warped and malfunctional society. If Tina was seeing her mother accepting abuse and performing sexual acts to please abusive violent males, how could she not see these act as normal behaviour? Hence, psychotherapy was doomed to fail from the outset. Two hours per week with a therapist cannot cancel the rest of the time spent in a warped environment. If we want to change the maladaptive behaviour, we need to deal with its source.

In contrast, it is hard to judge if, in fact, Tina had significantly benefited from her interaction with the therapist. Her weekly visits to the clinic might have provided her with protection from further sexual abuse or violence, but it is difficult to measure the therapy's true impact on her. Over the years, one comes to appreciate that science often deals only in probabilities.

'I'M NOT THE SAME SINCE I LOST MY DAD'

Ahmad was referred to psychotherapy after being diagnosed with anxiety. Initially, he spoke about his marital problems and successful career as a policeman. He also complained about struggling with insomnia, lack of joy, anxiety and intrusive thoughts of death. During the first session, he kept bringing up his father's death and the profound impact it had had on him. He repeated general statements such as, 'It's a tragedy to lose your father. If you lose your father, you lose everything. My father's in heaven now and he's happy, and I should pray for him. He's happier than me.'

In the second and third sessions, Ahmad continued to talk about his marital problems and how his wife wanted to leave him, and again spoke about his father's death. At the same time, he complained of sadness, anxiety and fear of death. He described his fears when he thought of death, his heart palpitations and shortness of breath. He said that his mental condition was hurting everyone around him, including his wife, and he did not blame her if she wanted to divorce him. It made him sad he could not play with his daughters, since he had no energy and was unable even to force himself to smile. Sometimes, he would scream at and scare them, and then regret it. His wife would accuse him of being a bad father, and this left him devastated.

In the fourth session, Ahmad started by praising the therapist. He repeated several times that he felt good and believed the therapy and medication were helping him a great deal. He was also sleeping better. There was a long pause and Ahmad's body language suggested he expected affirmation that the therapy was a success. However, nothing of that sort took place, as self-praise and premature evaluation are not part of psychotherapy. The therapist's assessment showed that, at that point, a rapport with the patient was not fully developed, and observation of Ahmad indicated that his situation, if anything, had deteriorated. His affect was cold, he appeared upset and absent-minded, and his hand gestures, facial expressions, voice tone and clothes all indicated he was not improving. His obvious weight gain was another marker that could not be missed.

As the session neared its end, Ahmad abruptly shifted the topic to discussing his feelings towards his late father. He said in a loud and assertive voice, 'Everyone must love their father, right? We must love, obey and adore our parents regardless of what they did to us. It's God's command to respect and love our parents, especially fathers, right?'

The therapist did not respond.

Then Ahmad asked in a calm but tense voice, 'Why don't you answer me? Am I right?'

The therapist replied, 'We don't give answers to things we don't know. It's up to you to say if you love your father or not. It's only you who can talk about your feelings.'

Interrupting the therapist, Ahmad screamed, 'I hate him! I hate him so much, I wish he was alive so I could kill him with my bare hands. I regret not confronting him... I know I shouldn't say that. It's the first time I've said such a thing. A psychologist I saw last year told me it's wrong to say I didn't really love my father. He told me I should respect my father regardless of what he'd done to me, but I can't help it. I really can't.'

Ahmed went on to reveal painful details of his father's abusive behaviour. 'He married my mother as his second wife when he was 50 and she was 15. She came from a poor refugee family and her father sold her to my father. He already had six children with his first wife. He used to beat my mother up savagely. He enjoyed beating her and us in public. He would beat us for no reason. He would call me a son of a whore and a bastard in front of my friends.

'One day, it was Eid, and I was so happy that day. I was 11 years old, playing in the street with other kids from the neighbourhood. Suddenly, my father pulled over, calling out loudly. I ran to him as my friends watched. He slapped and spat on me. I fell to the ground, the world spinning around me. I was crying uncontrollably and wet my pants. Even now, at 40 years of age, I recall this moment as if it happened this morning – the shame, fear and anger. I remember how at that moment I wanted to kill him. I remember the faces of my friends. They were shocked and upset; one boy cried loudly when he saw what happened to me.

'As I lay on the ground, my father got out of the car and started kicking me with his foot. He stepped on my head with his dirty shoes. I ran away, but kept hearing his voice calling me "son of a whore", "faggot", "idiot". I can't forget the sorrow in my friends' eyes. Their looks cut deeper than the beating. To this day, when I see one of those guys, I avoid him. One has become a policeman and was recently transferred to my workplace. I immediately asked my boss to change my working hours: I was willing to work the night shift all week rather than see this guy. I was afraid he might tell the others about my father and how he treated me. I was relieved when he left the police station. I'm sure he did it out of kindness towards me.

'When I was 15, I begun standing up to my father, trying to protect my mother from his beatings. I was still small and very skinny, and he was much more powerful but I think I was brave. One day, I found her on the floor and he was standing on top of her, punching her face and whipping her with a belt. She was screaming but would not defend herself. I came running and pushed him away. He fled like a coward. He was evil but a coward. He would smile while pretending to be upset. He called my half-brother, who was 23, and ordered him to hit me with a stick he gave him. My brother hit me over the head. I fell to the ground. My father came holding a belt and whipped me while I was on the floor. My mother stood and watched without interfering.

'After that incident, I ran away from home. I was lucky that one of the neighbours took me in. A few months later, my father came to the man's house screaming. He told him to throw me out, saying I was a bastard and not his son. The neighbour told him to go away and never speak to him again.

'My father went to the police, and they called the decent man. They asked me about why I didn't want to go with my father. When I told them he beat and abused me, they yelled at me and called me ungrateful. If it were not for the neighbour who interfered and took me with him, they might have forced me to go with my father.

'Despite the fact that I really love the man who sheltered me, I couldn't bring myself to visit him. Once I left his house when I was 18, I did not go back even once. I know he loved me, and I'm sure that he knows how grateful I am for all that he has done for me. He was more of a father to me than my biological parents ever were. He taught me many things and didn't expect anything in return, and never got anything. I joined the police force when I was 17. Once I had a steady income, my mother started contacting me, asking for money. When I was 18, I rented a room and was spending all my time at work. Did you know – in the police station, there are beds and there is always food, and people around?

'When I was 25, I met my wife. She was incredibly kind to me and, like me, she had suffered from an abusive father and a complicit mother. I hadn't seen my father for 13 years before his death. Since his death, my mother has been pressuring me to give her money and to divorce my wife. She even suggested that my daughter might not be mine and that I should do a DNA test.

'I hate them. I refuse to give them money. I refuse to pray for them. I refuse to visit my father's grave; in fact, I want to spit on it. Am I crazy? Am I mentally ill?'

Ahmad continued with his psychotherapy and consistently took his medication. He was highly motivated to improve himself and overcome his troubles. Over time, his improvement was obvious. He started spending more time with his family and cut his relationships with many people. He begun expressing his feelings to close friends and siblings. When comparing his reaction, emotions and the way he talked about himself and his troubles in recent to early sessions, there was clear improvement.

The psychiatrist gradually reduced his medication dosage before stopping it completely, and the psychotherapy concluded a few months later. It would not be fair to attribute the success solely to medication and psychotherapy: Ahmad himself played a critical role. He did not miss a session. He diligently took his medication. He started exercising and went back to carpentry, which he loved. Moreover, he pushed himself to resist the intrusive thoughts and irrational urges, devising ways to keep himself busy and content.

'MY OLDER BROTHER LOST HIS MIND'

An old friend contacted me asking for help with his brother, whom he claimed had 'lost his mind'. I had only vague memories of his brother – a boring, pretentious man, a few years older than us, who was an army officer. I recall he had a huge wedding when I was a university student. He always dressed formally and spoke in a pompous tone. As I awaited his arrival in my office, a man wearing shorts, an earring, a cut-off t-shirt and trainers walked in. He greeted me but I could not immediately place him.

'Khalid?' I asked.

'Yes,' he replied.

Moments later, his brother followed. He did not speak. Not sure how to proceed, I asked my friend to wait outside. I began some small talk with Khalid before moving on to explain the rules and ethical regulations governing our meeting. After the pleasantries, Khalid paused and then spoke.

'Am I crazy for wanting to live my own life? Unlike you or my brother, I've never made my own choices until now. Before I finished high school, my father arranged for me to join the army college to become an officer. It's a great career and everyone wishes to be accepted. My family were happy for me, so I was happy. I never discussed with myself or with others whether I was a good fit for such a career. Would I enjoy it? Why am I joining the army? Many of my colleagues were extremely happy, but for me, it was mundane. I didn't care much for it. People were fighting over which branch of the army they wanted to join, what kind of gun they would be given. I was the easy-going one. Now, I think that I did not really care that much for it.

63

'By the time I was finishing my fourth and final year, many of my colleagues were already engaged. I had no one. My mother arranged for me to marry one of her relatives, after seeking the girl's parents' approval. One weekend, I came home to a celebratory atmosphere, complete with cake and music, and everyone congratulated me. "Congrats – the girl's parents have agreed for her to marry you." I still remember being numb at that moment. I was not upset or happy. I was just numb. It was as if I were watching a film or listening to a story. Something that didn't really concern me.

'Then I was busy with the wedding arrangements. It was a traditional marriage. I'd seen the girl a few times before the marriage. I barely knew her. We went to Miami for the honeymoon. It was great. We stayed at a five-star hotel. We went on many excursions, and things were fine, just fine. I just couldn't help noticing that my wife looked like one of my uncles. She had the same chin, eyes and laugh. I've never liked that macho uncle. She was thin, and he was morbidly obese, which made the resemblance less obvious but she did look and act like him.

'Nine months after the wedding, my first daughter was born, a beautiful girl who looked like my sister. It was a joy for me. I took her wherever I went. A year later, I had twin boys, and then another girl. So, I had four kids before I was 30. My life was hectic between hospitals, supermarkets, schools and my job. In my job, I was the no-one guy. I didn't compete for power, which meant I wasn't really noticed. My routine was set: a 9 to 5 job, then straight to the super-market, then off to the doctor if one of the kids was ill and then I'd meet my friends to smoke hookah and drink tea. By II, I would be home so I could sleep until 6. My week-ends were spent visiting my family or in-laws. Yes, I bought a piece of land and built a huge house. This kept me busy and financially and emotionally drained for several years.

'I don't know what happened last year. I turned 44, but I don't know what really happened. It's as if I'd been asleep and just woke up. There was a moment: I was sitting in my living room doing nothing while my wife was engrossed in her soap opera – it was then that clarity struck. I started admitting to myself that I really didn't like my job and I wasn't suited to be an officer. With my peaceful nature and weak personality, how on earth was I supposed to be a fighter? Everyone knew that I was not a real soldier!

'I remember, one day I was passing by a couple of soldiers and one of them asked his friend if they should stand up and do the military salute. The other told him not to worry about me. They didn't bother, and I pretended I didn't notice and hadn't heard what they'd said. Such a scenario would be unthinkable with any other officer.

'As for my wife, she has never shown me much affection. It was always about the house, the furniture, the kids, the meals – never about us. I doubt I have ever been in love, except maybe the crush I had on one of my neighbours. By the way, my wife now looks exactly like the uncle I told you about, although he's a bit thinner than her. My relationship with my kids is the only healthy thing: I love them, and my eldest daughter is a friend of mine. We even go shopping together.

'Once I realized that I was not happy with my life, I couldn't continue wearing the mask. I resigned from my job, left the house and now I wear these clothes and drive a red Camaro. Many people think I'm crazy but, for me, I'm experiencing things I never knew existed. I go to cafés, I go clubbing, I travel and I have new friends. I can't keep putting on the mask to please everyone while I'm miserable.'

65

'I AM FINE – I JUST NEED A LITTLE HELP'

All that glitters is not gold.

Shakespeare, *The Merchant of Venice*

'Doctor, I'm fine. I just sometimes don't feel well. You know the nature of my work, the social pressures and dealing with people – all that can be stressful. If possible, could you teach me some techniques or ways to cope with stress? Maybe you could recommend some types of meditation, a self-help book or yoga classes to help me feel better and be more productive and at peace with myself. I see a psychiatrist who gave me Prozac [an antidepressant]; it's helping but I think it's not enough. I've seen some life coaches who taught me ways to deal with my stress but I feel I need some short and effective psychotherapy.'

This was what Omar told the therapist during their first meeting. He explained to Omar that if he was truly fine, psychotherapy was not what he needed. Therapists are not in a position to tell people how to live their lives. People are capable of finding ways to improve their mood and make themselves happy if they want to. They can try studying, meditation, yoga, sports or any other activity they choose.

Psychotherapy, both medication and talk therapy, is designed to help people with mental disorders gain insight into their condition and manage their symptoms. The job of psychotherapists is to provide a safe environment for patients to discuss their problems and feelings. They are responsible for establishing a professional relationship with the patients to allow them to speak freely and understand themselves without fear of being judged. Psychotherapists must ensure that patients are not a threat to themselves or others. They are not there to prescribe lifestyles, give orders or influence decisions of their patients.

Omar continued coming to the clinic. It turned out that he had been admitted to a mental hospital and had spent a few nights there at the age of 12. After several sessions, it became clear that Omar suffers from obsessive compulsive disorder. His disorder manifests in repeated praying and washing before praying. For many years, Omar managed to conceal his illness. The symptoms came and went. At times, he felt better, with fewer intrusive thoughts and less painful compulsions – their effect on his daily life was tolerable. However, at other times, especially during stressful periods, his symptoms would flare up and reach a point where he could no longer conceal or tolerate them.

As a devoted Muslim, Omar is obliged to pray five times a day. The first prayer must be performed at dawn, followed by noon, afternoon, sunset and evening prayers. Before each prayer, one must perform a specific washing ritual. Failing to wash properly means the prayer is invalid and must be repeated. Omar would wake up an hour before sunrise to wash and prepare for the dawn prayer. Sometimes, he found himself repeating the washing rituals multiple times, and then he would repeat the prayers, until he was exhausted and would miss work. On some days, he would stop praying because he was late for work or too exhausted to carry on. He would usually tell himself he would redo the washing and prayer rituals once he returned home. On a bad day, he would spend most of his time washing, praying, crying and blaming himself.

Omar's thoughts would escalate from obsessing over performing prayers correctly to believing he was incapable of washing and praying because God did not like him. His intrusive thoughts kept growing more complex. He started from believing that God did not want his prayers to the notion that he would end up in hellfire because he did not pray or wash properly. He felt inferior to his siblings who did not care about prayer as much. He stopped travelling and began living in a separate room from his wife because he did not want her to see him crying and slapping his face. After years of psychodynamic therapy to help him understand himself and the cause of his problem better, a comprehensive understanding of Omar's case was reached.

He grew up in a religious household with extremely strict and abusive parents. His father often beat his children with various objects, his favourite being a hose, and would whip them for the smallest mistake. His parents were obsessed with prayer. As the eldest, Omar was taught to pray from an early age. To pray, he had to wash first, and his father would wake him before dawn every day for this ritual.

As a child, Omar would often splash water on his clothes, which his mother considered a major crime. She was obsessed with cleanliness and prayer, and would scream at him for being 'filthy'. Hence, he could not pray and, most importantly, rendered any place unsuitable for prayer, according to her beliefs. If she thought he had not washed properly, she would beat him savagely, with his father joining in.

From the age of 10, Omar became increasingly stressed about praying, washing and staying clean. Sometimes, he would stay in the bathroom for hours trying to clean himself, causing him to be late for school, which would result in more beatings from his father. From an early age, his parents instilled in him a fear of hellfire, warning him that disobedience, neglecting prayer or not fasting would lead to eternal damnation. They also instilled in him a fear of demons and death, frequently telling him stories about the tortures awaiting sinners after death. These fears led to constant nightmares about the grave, death and hellfire. He used to wet his bed, which invited more beatings and humiliation from his parents.

One day, Omar lost control and started screaming hysterically. Then he had a fit. His father's screaming and beating did not stop him: he fell to the ground, shaking and convulsing. His parents took him to the emergency department of their local hospital, where he was referred to a mental hospital. The doctors decided to keep him there to protect him from his abusive parents. At that time, there were no effective ways to protect children from abusive parents, a situation still widespread across the Middle East. Beating and abusing children is often seen as normal practice.

The doctors told Omar's parents to stop hitting him and forcing him to pray. They had to lie and tell the parents he was mentally ill and that forcing him to pray would make him lose his mind. They suggested the parents wait for him to grow up before he could resume prayer. The parents, though unconvinced, relaxed their treatment of Omar, but remained strict with their other children.

After his release from the hospital, Omar was treated as abnormal and was mainly kept at home due to the stigma attached to mental illness in the Middle East. He used his time to study and read, achieving good grades and developing his skills. He studied law and became a respected judge known for his ethics and decency. However, he never ceased to suffer. He developed obsessive-compulsive behaviour. He would spend hours every day washing, praying

69

and praying again. He was plagued by intrusive thoughts that he had not washed properly, making him repeat the process. Sometimes, he would interrupt his prayer to wash again and start over. He struggled for years, but his condition worsened over time.

He was married in an arranged marriage to a simple woman he did not love, though he cared for her. As his life fell apart, he sought help. Despite being married, he had no passionate relationship with his wife, and his relationship with his children was strained. He would spend his nights praying and crying, tormented by intrusive thoughts. He thought he was condemned to a life in hellfire. If his prayer was not accepted, then everything else was invalid. His marriage was invalid because he was not a true believer, since he did not pray correctly. If his marriage was invalid, then his children were illegitimate, and they should not carry his name. Before seeking therapy, Omar had attempted to take his life several times.

Chapter 4.
Irrational beliefs and their cost

Negative thought patterns, unresolved conflicts and irrational beliefs are the main psychological causes of mood disorder, according to psychological theories. In this chapter, I will highlight some irrational patterns of thought I have found to be extremely harmful. These patterns are not only related to mental disorders but also cause avoidable suffering and are often promoted by powerful institutions and influential figures.

HAVING KIDS IS A BURDEN AND LIVING ALONE IS BEAUTIFUL

Journalist and author Petronella Wyatt penned an insightful article titled 'Feminism Has Left Middle-Aged Women Like Me Single, Childless, and Depressed' (The Telegraph, 2024). In it, she explains how intelligent, ambitious women have been persuaded by the elites that to be successful and important they needed to forgo marriage, family and having children. As a result, about 10 per cent of British women in their 50s have never been married, have no children and live alone. This situation is mirrored across the Western world and among the highly educated globally. This leaves these intelligent people victims of loneliness and lacking social support networks – major factors in mental disorders and lower quality of life. Additionally, society loses their genes and suffers from low birth rates.

Petronella writes about her own experience and that of her friends, highlighting how they are suffering from depression and loneliness. She does so in an extremely kind and selfless way, aiming to warn the new generation against making the same mistakes:

> According to a recent study by an American medical institute, loneliness is the leading cause of depression among middle-aged females. I should know, as I recently fell prey to the unforgiving maw of mental illness. This has taken me to hospital several times after I experienced impulses so dark that friends became concerned. On one occasion, I recall a nurse in A&E [Accident and Emergency] asking me about my plans to end my life, and replying that, like Keir Starmer's views on women, they were unformed. But the truth is that much of my depression sprang from a solitary existence that would be eschewed by a race of alley cats. I do not know one single woman of my generation who lives such a life and actually likes it.

Having studied and worked in different universities and institutions, I unfortunately became disillusioned with activist elites quite late. Several academics I once admired for their honesty, opposition to the status quo and animosity toward big corporations – famous, influential intellectuals teaching at prestigious universities – now advocate for dismantling the family institution. They argue that liberating women starts with cancelling marriage and forgoing having children. Many of these intellectuals, who write books and lecture about freedom and equality, condemn traditional society and Western civilization. They fervently defend abortion and present it as the right course without discussing the mental health consequences to the individual or the broader social and economic consequences of abortion and not having a spouse, partner or children.

Over the years, I have observed how old men use revolutionary, passionate rhetoric to attract young women and to maintain a steady income, not just in politics but also in academia, medicine and literature. All they really seem to care about is earning large sums without much effort, having relationships with multiple women and exploiting gullible flocks of followers. Typically, these men appeal to intelligent, ambitious, compassionate, yet inexperienced, young women who aspire to make a difference in the world. They convince them that the world needs more fighters for justice, encouraging them to surrender their brains to the aged hucksters who benefit from talking about justice. These men have created a dominant rhetoric designed to convince women to disdain having children because children will hinder their future.

Young people often lack enough information and do not understand the consequences of their decisions. Awareness of the nature of these decisions and their consequences is an essential component of freedom. It is the duty of society and intellectuals to explain in detail to young people the pros and cons of having children, aborting a child and establishing a family. Moreover, it is crucial that the debate is not dominated by self-serving individuals who have a stranglehold on the media.

THE GAY GYNAECOLOGIST

The street where I lived at one point in my life used to be a residential area for members of the Communist Party, who had been in power for decades after World War II. I met a number of them, but none impressed me, despite their numerous titles and past glories. They were all old men reciting memorized clichés, and never speaking in a direct way. One of them, however, was particularly interesting. He was a gay man who had been married to women twice and had three children. He was a gynaecologist. His house was one of the most impressive villas I have ever seen: a three-storey building with a beautiful garden, right in the middle of the city. When he found out I was a psychologist, he insisted on meeting me. We had several discussions, and he always asked about my views on abortion and why it was illegal in the Middle East. He believed it was a healthcare issue and a woman's right. 'Men have no say in abortion,' he would emphasize.

The way he insisted on bringing up this topic repeatedly, becoming aggressive and emotional each time, was hard to ignore. Neighbours, who were my friends, seemed unhappy about my visiting this man, but no one was willing to be frank about it or tell me why. One evening, the discussion became especially heated as the American Supreme Court had just overturned Roe versus Wade, a landmark ruling. He was furious, while I was pleased. When he asked why I was happy, I explained that I believe society needs to reconsider its stance on many issues, including abortion. In my view, we have swung from one extreme to another – from banning abortion even when necessary to making it the norm. Many people are pressured into abortion without the chance to make their own informed decisions.

The complex relationship between abortion and childlessness, on the one hand, and mental health issues, on the other, is rarely discussed and explained to the general public. Several studies have reported a strong link between abortion and mental disorders. A 30-year-long study conducted in Denmark showed that women and girls who choose to have an abortion may already have higher levels of mental health issues before the abortion. The study found that, among the women and girls who chose to have an abortion, nearly four times as many had previously sought help from psychiatric services compared to those who carried their pregnancies to term and gave birth.

In my practice, I have encountered many patients traumatised by abortion. One of the first inpatients I saw as a junior psychologist was a striking woman who had just turned 50. She had been brought in by the police after harassing students playing football on a university campus. The students reported that she would watch them and occasionally chase them. One day, in a state of agitation and hysteria, the police were called. Distressed, she was taken to the mental health institution where she was already an outpatient. She had been diagnosed with clinical depression for many years.

In psychotherapy, it emerged that her ex-boyfriend had pressured her to abort when she was 20 and he was 27. They stayed together for a further ten years. He wanted to focus on his career and saw children as an obstacle. Eventually, he started seeing another woman and left her. Now, he is married with three daughters and lives in a beautiful house, while she returns every night to her rented one-bedroom apartment. She has put on weight, stopped taking care of herself and is lonely. She repeatedly said that if she had kept the child, who would have been an adult by now, her life would have been different.

She used to drive to the university campus where she spent hours watching the young students. On that day, she had a nervous breakdown, crying out, 'I want my son back. I want to see him at the university. I want him to introduce me to his friends. I want him to drive me around. I could have had a handsome boy.' She was admitted to the hospital, and her medications had to be increased.

Over the years, I have met many women who have gone through similar experiences. Their stories underscore the deep and lasting impact that deciding to abort can have on a person's mental health. This case in particular highlights the need for society to approach the topic of abortion with greater sensitivity and support for those affected.

Another case involved a friend of mine who had lost several children conceived with different women. He never really agreed to the abortions but was too afraid to speak his mind and express the desire to be a father. 'If I had had any of those kids, I would have been happy,' he repeats whenever the topic comes up.

One of his ex-girlfriends, years after they had separated, confided in him that she had been depressed and on medication for many years. She told him that her sister, with a modest job and no postgraduate degree, has a caring husband, two beautiful children and four grandchildren. The sister's birthday, marriage anniversary, and her husband's birthday are important events celebrated by her family, who love and cherish her. In comparison, my friend's ex-girlfriend, with a PhD and significant professional achievements, now feels pressured into retirement by former students half her age, and feels she has nothing and nobody. 'Why did we not keep that child?' she asked him.

As I was narrating these stories, the gynaecologist from my street was getting more upset. He revealed that many people saw him as a monster and child killer. He confessed to having a secret clinic in his basement, where he performed abortions. Senior Communist Party members would send him girls they got pregnant. Many of these girls were underage; others were married women. All were vulnerable. The man told me he didn't feel good about himself. He kept repeating: 'It was their choice.'

LONELINESS IS HELL

One of the most harmful myths perpetuated as a solution to our problems is that other people and committed relationships are bad, and that solitude and open relationships are ideal. Many authors and thinkers still echo Jean-Paul Sartre's famous line 'Hell is other people,' without considering his other absurd claims such as 'the Soviet Union is a total democracy without elections', 'Man is a useless passion' who is 'condemned to be free' and 'We have never been so free as under the German occupation.'

Sartre's quote 'Hell is other people,' from his play *No Exit*, reflects the existentialist view that much of our suffering comes from how we perceive ourselves through others' eyes, which leads to living inauthentic lives and conflicts in interpersonal relationships. In the play, three characters are condemned to an eternity together in a room, where their torment stems from constant judging and the inability to escape each other's scrutiny. This situation shows how reliance on external validation, conforming to social expectations and the inevitable clashes in human relationships create a personal 'hell'. Sartre's existentialism emphasises personal responsibility and authenticity, suggesting that true freedom lies in embracing our own choices and defining ourselves independently of external judgement.

However, despite Sartre's philosophical contributions and stature as a celebrated intellectual and role model, he serves as a prime example of the failure of elites in choosing and promoting genuine thinkers. Sartre's ideas are often little more than recycled ancient arguments without evidence or practical application.

Moreover, Sartre's support for mass murderers such as Stalin, Mao Zedong and Fidel Castro is well documented. Throughout his life, he aligned himself with cruel dictators, ignoring the suffering of their victims while claiming to champion freedom and humanity. He glossed over the horrific crimes committed by these regimes, demonstrating a blatant disregard for truth, human dignity and intellectual integrity. Sartre's ideological blindness reveals a disturbing willingness to excuse tyranny in the name of philosophical purity.

In his personal life, Sartre's relationships were anything but successful or ethical. He seduced many students half his age, used them and then discarded them at will. His long-term open relationship with Simone de Beauvoir, an equally unethical person, involved both of them exploiting underage students, as recounted in memoirs, biographies and scholarly works. Bianca Lamblin, one of the students involved with Sartre and de Beauvoir, wrote about the manipulative nature of their relationships in her

Mémoires d'une Jeune Fille Dérangée. She described how she was seduced by de Beauvoir at 17 and later passed on to Sartre, highlighting the power dynamics and emotional abuse she suffered.

Despite his vibrant public life, Sartre's final years were marked by profound loneliness as people started to see his reality. He spent his last years sick, childless and dependent on others' help. The absence of a close-knit family or lasting friendships left him isolated, a stark contrast to his earlier life filled with intellectual companionship and public admiration. This later period underscores the emptiness of a life devoid of genuine, supportive relationships.

Sartre's claim 'Hell is other people' misses the true sources of existential anguish: hypocrisy, confusion, immoral people and loneliness. His life was riddled with contradictions, from his political stances to his personal relationships. This hypocrisy undermines his philosophical claims and reveals a disconnect between his words and actions.

Sartre's praise for the Soviet Union reveals a deep confusion about political and social realities, resulting in flawed actions and beliefs that cause personal and societal turmoil. Interactions with genuinely evil or immoral individuals can create a personal hell far more intense than the mere presence of others. Sartre's manipulative behaviour towards his young lovers is an example of the harmfulness of bad people.

Ultimately, Sartre's later life demonstrates that true hell may lie in the absence of meaningful connections. Despite being surrounded by people, his failure to cultivate lasting, supportive relationships left him deeply isolated in the end. Sartre's life serves as a stark reminder that human connections, despite their complexities and challenges, are essential to our well-being. Rather than avoiding others, we can seek to build relationships grounded in mutual respect and understanding, recognizing that our shared humanity can be a source of strength and comfort.

VICTIMIZATION

One method employed by corrupt politicians to stay in power is dividing society into fighting groups. Among the most used notions are the divisions between oppressors and the oppressed, the evil and the good, the rich and the poor. Politicians can then win election or popular support by presenting themselves as the ones maintaining the balance or trying to amend the exaggerated injustices. However, framing people, particularly minorities, as victims of systemic injustice has deleterious effects on them and can lead to a broken society.

Thomas Sowell, a prominent economist and social theorist, in his book *Race and Culture*, extensively critiques the victimization narrative. He argues that this mindset undermines personal responsibility and agency, creating a culture where individuals do not feel accountable for their actions. According to Sowell, the constant reinforcement of victimhood can lead to a culture of dependency, where individuals wait for others to help them rather than taking steps to improve their circumstances.

One of the key issues with the victimization narrative is its potential to absolve individuals of personal responsibility. When people believe their failures or hardships are due solely to external factors beyond their control, they may feel justified in not striving to overcome those obstacles. This mindset can be particularly damaging to minorities who, despite facing genuine challenges, possess the potential to succeed through determination and hard work.

In the United States, for example, the Black community has faced significant historical and systemic disadvantages. However, Sowell, in his later book *Black Rednecks and White Liberals*, points out that many successful Black individuals and communities have thrived despite these obstacles. He argues that emphasizing personal responsibility and resilience is crucial for overcoming adversity. For instance, during the early twentieth century, Black educational institutions and businesses flourished even under oppressive conditions. In contrast, when the notion that Black people are perpetual victims and cannot achieve much took hold, it led to an increase in poverty, crime, teenage pregnancy, and the breakdown of family structures.

Data supports the idea that a victim mindset can be harmful. A study by the Pew Research Center, published in 2016, found that African Americans who believe in hard work are more likely to become successful than those who feel that racial discrimination is the primary barrier to their advancement. This suggests that focusing on personal agency and effort can yield better outcomes than a focus on victimization.

In the United Kingdom, similar patterns are observed. The British Social Attitudes survey, published in 2017, showed that individuals from minority backgrounds who view themselves as victims of systemic racism are less likely to engage in civic activities and more likely to experience feelings of helplessness. This lack of engagement in societal structures that could facilitate positive change is worrying.

Furthermore, the constant narrative of victimization can create a divided society. When people are continually told they are victims, it can foster resentment and hostility towards their perceived oppressors, exacerbating social tensions. This division is counterproductive to building a cohesive and inclusive society.

The impact on mental health is also significant. Studies have shown that individuals who see themselves as victims are more likely to experience anxiety, depression and other mental health issues. For example, a study by David Williams and others published in the *Journal of Health and Social Behaviour* in 2012 found that perceived discrimination is linked to increased psychological distress among minority groups.

In conclusion, while it is essential to recognize and address genuine injustices, perpetuating the narrative of victimization can have adverse effects on individuals and society. It can undermine personal responsibility, foster dependency and create social divisions. By acknowledging personal agency, ambition, realistic understanding and focusing on overcoming obstacles, people can achieve their potential.

A WRONG DIAGNOSIS

Ruth worked at a college where I regularly gave talks. She had an undeniable presence: her femininity and appeal were impossible to ignore. Though she was not particularly tall, her long hair cascaded down her back and framed her curvaceous body, and the way she moved added to her magnetic charm. Every time I visited to give a talk, she would attend and often volunteer to organise the event. Beyond her striking looks, Ruth was a deeply serious and intelligent person, well versed in psychology, philosophy and many other topics. She usually wore short skirts but always covered her arms with long sleeves. I could not help but notice what looked like cut marks on her arms, starting from the back of her hands. She was very particular about covering them.

One day, she called and asked if she could see me in my clinic. When she arrived, she was pale, her elegant clothes and makeup unable to mask the traces of recent tears. As soon as she sat down, she broke into sobs. At that moment, she appeared more like a fragile, vulnerable girl than the poised and captivating woman I had come to know.

'I am going through a bad time. I feel so desperate and upset with myself. I ended my relationship with my fiancé. I'm not sad about the breakup, although perhaps I should be. I'm sad that I let it drag on for all that time. He was bullying me and calling me names. What started as love at first sight ended in bullying and harassment. I wanted to end the relationship a long time ago – in fact, after the first two months I realised it was going nowhere. Every time I decided to end it, I would talk myself out of it or consult with someone who would convince me otherwise. I wasted two years of my life for nothing. I hurt myself and allowed him to demean me for nothing. I think he felt the same way. He was as fed up with me as I was with him. He started ignoring me, calling me an idiot, crazy, psycho and a bitch. At first, he would do it when we fought, but later he would say these things without any reason, sometimes even jokingly. He kept pointing out my scars.

'I'm not here seeking psychotherapy; I'm here because I want to have a candid conversation. My problems started when I was around 16. My body developed suddenly. My breasts grew and my figure changed. I could tell I looked much older and more feminine than my friends. Suddenly, the skinny, petite girl turned into Marilyn Monroe. Guys would drool when they saw me. Big, important, respected men would become kids when they spoke to me.

'At that time, my parents were separating. It was a nasty and traumatizing experience that affected us all. My mother loved my dad but didn't treat him well. He was a gentleman – an intellectual and a sensitive man, a true citizen of the world. He was well travelled, elegant, smart, spoke several languages, played music and enjoyed poetry. She was a good-looking, simple woman, kind and intelligent, but not on my father's level. When they met, she was fascinated by him and wanted to share his interests and hobbies but, over time, she changed her mind. She immersed herself in trivial, silly things. She refused to go to music concerts with him, and she hated travelling, camping and hiking. While he always had a heavy book in his hand, she never touched a book, except for cookbooks.

'He stayed with her for the sake of their two daughters. When I was 14 and my older sister was 16, he grew tired of putting up with her. I think that was when he fell in love with my stepmother. The two were cut from the same cloth. They were both trapped in miserable marriages. They met at a conference and wanted to be together. My father was very honest. He told my mother he couldn't continue in the marriage and thought it was best to separate. My mum exploded. She became vengeful, intent on destroying my father and us with him, which she did. She started fighting with my father and his family, even going to his workplace to embarrass him in front of his employees. She hired a nasty lawyer, who ruined my father's reputation, accusing him of hitting her and stealing her money. My mother accused my dad of abusing his daughters and coerced us to testify in court. But still, all that my mum did was fruitless. In the end, my father married the woman he loved and regained the respect of society. My mother is the one who lost her reputation and is now seen as a liar and crazy. She had a short relationship with that despicable lawyer, then she married a sleazy older man and got a divorce. To this day, she still accuses my father of immoral things. She sometimes even says that I'm like my father – an arrogant bastard.

'After my parents divorced and my father moved away, I started hurting myself. I'd keep cutting my hands until the blood covered the whole bed, and I'd faint. I'd wake up in the hospital with all these doctors trying to understand why I did this to myself.

'My journey began with mental hospitals and psychological clinics, preachers, con artists and all the nosy people who want to control everyone else... It was a long, tedious journey that consumed my life. I wasted years pretending to be sick and listening to people spouting nonsense.

'I was enjoying the attention. My father was spending more time with me, buying me things he could barely afford, things I didn't really need. He felt guilty for leaving and blamed himself for what had happened to me. My mother was less abusive: she also felt guilty. I was getting gifts and money from everyone. I was seeing older guys, and I enjoyed their interest in me. I was diagnosed with borderline personality disorder. In reality, I was a confused teenager craving attention. Several therapists and psychologists who dealt with me were unethical. One told me to give him a hug, saying that's what I needed. He was a sleazy old man, and I was a 16-year-old girl. Another therapist used to scream at me, calling me indecent. Another professed his love, promising to make me the happiest person on earth if I agreed to date him. Many others didn't care much about me: to them, I was just another case. They searched for symptoms and, once found, they were ready to write the same prescriptions as always. I read about these symptoms and became an expert at role-playing. I would exaggerate my distress, my thoughts, my behaviour, and convince myself that I was sick and needed help.

'I believe if the first therapist I saw had been firm and told my father that I was normal and that he shouldn't encourage my behaviour, things would have been different. I wish my father had given me attention regardless of my inappropriate behaviour rather than because of it.'

'WE ARE ALL SICK AND NEED HELP'

In recent decades, there has been a massive surge in the diagnosis of conditions such as attention deficit hyperactivity disorder (ADHD), depression and anxiety all over the world. A 2019 report by the British National Health Service (NHS) indicated a 25 per cent increase in the number of children diagnosed with ADHD over five years, with many experts arguing that normal childhood behaviours are often mislabelled as mental illness.

Similarly, the Royal College of Psychiatrists in 2018 raised concerns about the overdiagnosis of depression and anxiety, noting that mild symptoms are frequently treated with medication rather than lifestyle changes or therapy. Studies have also highlighted concerns about the misdiagnosis of conditions such as bipolar disorder, with misdiagnosis rates ranging from 40 to 70 per cent. In 2018, approximately 1.9 million adults in the UK were diagnosed with ADHD, sparking debates on overdiagnosis.

Australia faces similar issues, with research from the University of Sydney, published in 2014, indicating that approximately 20 per cent of patients diagnosed with mental health conditions such as depression and anxiety may not meet the clinical criteria for these. This over-diagnosis can lead to inappropriate treatments and un-necessary exposure to medication side effects. Additionally, around 30 per cent of patients with depression were found to be misdiagnosed, often due to overlapping symptoms with other disorders.

In the USA, according to a 2016 Centers for Disease Control and Prevention (CDC) report, the number of ADHD diagnoses in children had increased by over 40 per cent in the previous decade, raising concerns about overdiagnosis and overmedication. A study published in the *Journal of the American Medical Association* in 2011 found that up to 26 per cent of adults diagnosed with depression may not meet the criteria for major depressive disorder. The National Institute of Mental Health (NIMH) estimates that more than one in five US adults has a mental illness (57.8 million in 2021). Yet, many researchers argue that this high number results from the phenomenon of pathologisation, where people are either misdiagnosed or overdiagnosed.

Pathologisation has become normalised in this era, where an endless stream of clinicians, dietitians, medical doctors and other health professionals argue that we must be ill in one way or another. In many cases, normal human experiences and behaviours are categorised as medical conditions requiring intervention.

A striking example is the increase in the number of post-traumatic stress disorder (PTSD) patients and individuals on sick leave. According to a study published in 2016 in the *Journal of Traumatic Stress*, the number of PTSD cases in the general population rose from 4.6 per cent in 2001–2003 to 6.8 per cent in 2012–2013. Furthermore, the World Health Organization in 2019 reported a 20 per cent increase in the number of individuals on sick leave due to mental-health issues over a ten-year period from 2009 to 2019.

If you belong to a minority group, have been through severe experiences or are experiencing discomfort, there is a growing tendency to assume that you must be suffering from some form of psychological illness and thus need professional help. For example, a study by the American Psychological Association published in 2013 found that racial minorities are more likely to be diagnosed with PTSD compared to Whites, not necessarily because of higher trauma exposure but due to greater clinical suspicion.

This trend raises important questions about finding the right balance between recognising legitimate health concerns and overmedicalizing everyday experiences. While awareness and treatment of genuine health issues are crucial, the tendency to label a wide range of behaviours and experiences as mental illness can lead to unnecessary medicalisation and a culture of dependence on professional health services.

The consequences of exaggerating mental ill health are serious. It can lead to overreliance on medication, as seen in the huge increase in antidepressant prescriptions. According to a 2011 CDC report, the use of antidepressants in the United States skyrocketed by nearly 400 per cent between 1988 and 1994 and between 2005 and 2008. Also, turning everyday-life challenges into medical issues can undermine people's resilience and ability to cope with stress and problems without professional help.

Moreover, this trend has broader societal impact, including increased healthcare costs and the risk of stigmatising those labelled as mentally ill. The overburdened healthcare system can become strained, diverting resources away from those who genuinely need medical help. The financial toll of mental health disorders is huge. For instance, a 2015 report from the NIMH estimated that major depression costs the US economy $210.5 billion annually.

In the UK, the number of individuals not working due to psychological issues is significant. According to the Health and Safety Executive, in 2019/2020, 828,000 workers suffered from work-related stress, depression or anxiety, leading to 17.9 million working days lost. This data underscores the heavy impact of mental health on employment and productivity.

A particularly telling example is the rise in diagnoses of ADHD. A 2016 report by the CDC indicates that the percentage of children diagnosed with ADHD increased from 7.8 per cent in 2003 to 11.0 per cent in 2011–2012. While awareness and diagnosis of ADHD are important, questions arise as to whether normal childhood behaviour is increasingly seen as abnormal.

In conclusion, while it is essential to recognise and address genuine health issues, misdiagnosing normal human experiences as abnormal can have significant negative consequences. It is crucial to find a balance that respects the complexity of human life without reducing it to a series of medical diagnoses. This balance involves fostering resilience, promoting healthy coping mechanisms and ensuring that medical intervention is reserved for those who genuinely need it, rather than broadly applying medical labels to everyday challenges.

MASS DELUSION: FROM EPICURUS TO CURRENT ACTIVISTS

> *Everyone thinks of changing the world, but no one thinks of changing himself.*
> Tolstoy

In a famous interview, Prince Harry said, 'Quitting brings joy.' He explained that, to prioritise their own happiness and mental health, many people leave jobs that do not bring them joy. Numerous responses to that comment pointed out that Prince Harry had never had a real job in his life. He lives in a mansion and is super-rich without getting a salary. The argument Harry made is not new. It brings to mind various self-help gurus who tell their audience to put themselves first and change whatever they do not like.

Avoiding stress to lead a happy life is one of the most influential notions promoted over the ages. It is part of an ancient debate that can be traced back to the Greek philosophy that investigated happiness, personal choice and the nature of society.

Epicurus, who dedicated his life to investigating happiness, which he saw as the main goal in life, concluded that reducing pain and increasing pleasure was the way to go. He argued that most people are incapable of achieving happiness due to false beliefs. In his view, people mistakenly believe that material gains such as fame, money and power are the best paths to happiness. However, the pursuit of wealth and power, he argued, leads to more anxiety and suffering.

Epicurus separated necessary from unnecessary desires, suggesting true happiness comes from fulfilling basic needs and enjoying simple, intellectual pleasures. He advocated for avoiding unnecessary stress and focusing on the pursuit of knowledge and friendship as essential elements of a happy life. According to Epicurus, all we need to be happy is freedom, a simple life surrounded by friends, self-sufficiency and time spent meditating, reading and contemplating ways to achieve tranquillity.

Epicurus established communes known as 'Gardens', where like-minded people could live together, sharing resources and supporting each other in the pursuit of a peaceful life. These communes were progressive for their time, accepting women and slaves, and centred around the principles of self-sufficiency, intellectual dialogue and mutual support. They were designed to provide a sanctuary from the distractions and corruptions of broader society. However, they were still a hierarchical institution, with Epicurus as the leader, who had given himself the title of 'the wise man'.

Epicurus emphasised the role friendship plays in our lives, arguing that having friends provides people with the security and help they need. In contrast, he did not support marriage, arguing that 'we leave ourselves open to troubles and inconveniences which may arise from wives and children we could otherwise avoid. So the wise man does not marry and have children.'

Epicurus and his followers faced strong criticism, not just from other philosophical schools but also from the general public. One major accusation was that they promoted hedonism and immorality. Critics argued that the Epicurean pursuit of pleasure led to a life of indulgence and moral decay. Epicurus was accused of leading young people away from traditional values and beliefs into a senseless existence with minimal contributions to society.

MARXISM IS THE CURE

It can be argued that communism is essentially a distorted version of Epicureanism blended with ideas from Plato's *Republic*. After all, Karl Marx studied Greek philosophy and wrote his doctoral thesis on the ideas of Democritus and Epicurus. The writings of Marx and Engels were especially attractive to frustrated people, as they offered a path to universal happiness – or so they claimed.

Karl Marx's writings serve as a prime example of how what is supposed to be a socio-economic theory has been used for decades as a one-size-fits-all immortal solution for the misfortunes of individuals and society. According to this view, people are unhappy because they are poor, and they are poor because they belong to the working class oppressed by the wealthy. Marx argued that once private ownership is abolished and everything is owned collectively by the proletariat, establishing a proletariat dictatorship, all the poor will have sufficient resources and thus be happy. In this ideal scenario, there would be no crimes or injustice, and people would go to work happy and excited. Everyone would be equal and content.

By deceiving people with this simplistic, misleading ideology, opportunists and dictators got into power, promising to use the teachings to create an earthly utopia. The result has been disastrous sadness, poverty and misery. The ideas of Marxism are extremely appealing for the following reasons:

» It contains some elements of truth.
» Certain parts are vague, which appeals to the human brain's love of mystery.
» It casts individuals as heroes: if you are poor or consider yourself part of the working class, you will be a leader of the proletariat.
» It offers simple solutions: there is injustice, and we can fix this injustice with laws and executive orders.
» It allows opportunists to satisfy their needs.
» It identifies and creates an enemy.

The former Soviet Union, China, North Korea and the communists of Europe and Africa have argued for decades that meeting minimal needs, creating a communist society controlled by its members and abolishing class distinctions and wealth inequalities lead to great happiness. But tragically, the deaths of millions in the Soviet Union, Romania, China, Cuba, Cambodia and North Korea as a result of the communist vision have failed to awaken many communists to the reality that their belief does not mesh with human nature. The ideals of communism cannot be achieved, as no society exists without a hierarchy or differences between people and their role in that society. No communist country has created or will create a society where everyone is happy.

To this day, multitudes around the world still defend the basic tenets of Marxism and Epicureanism. They hold on to the idea that we are all equal as humans, have the same needs, similar abilities and similar desires.

Currently, countless books and theories build upon a vision similar to Marx's, claiming that solving one's personal problems starts with changing society. Before the Iranian revolution in 1979, opponents of the monarchy told dissatisfied Iranian youth that all their problems stemmed from the Shah, his corrupt associates, his brutal secret police and the wealthy who exploited the poor. They promised that once the Shah was toppled, everyone would be free. They claimed Iran was the richest country in the world and would provide every Iranian with a huge house, a new car, and free medical care and education. Essentials such as petrol, electricity and running water would be free. Everyone would have whatever they desired, even without working. Many believed this propaganda, took to the streets and, eventually, the Shah was toppled.

The day after, a purge began to eliminate the members of the old regime and confiscate the wealth of those considered enemies of the revolution. The purge expanded to include many factions and individuals who had participated in the revolution, as well as all the elites and businessmen labelled as corrupt and opposed to the values of the revolution. Since 1979, well over 40 years ago, people have been waiting for the promised improvement in their lives, in vain.

The country lags in every aspect, lacking freedom of speech, an independent legal system and equality. Electricity and running water are not available in many areas, blackouts and long lines at petrol stations are common and the healthcare service is basic and not free. Millions have left the country, and millions more in Iran live in poverty. Despite this, countless people still argue that the revolution was justified, attributing the current suffering to enemies of the state and claiming that people must wait another 40 or 50 years to reap the fruits.

Totalitarian rationales, whether packaged as self-help books or political theories, are extremely dangerous and harmful, yet seductive. They claim that changing society is the first step to people finding a romantic partner or buying their own flat. They are appealing because they shift the blame for personal circumstances from the person to society. It is not you who cannot have a partner because you are lazy, fail to take care of yourself, do not have a decent job, do not study, do not go out and meet people or care about other people's feelings and rights. The ruling class suppresses you and, once it is toppled, you will suddenly look great and girls will be chasing after you.

Dream on! Even if you get rid of the regime and destroy your society's hierarchy, you will not achieve your personal goals. You are more likely to end up in a jail cell or a refugee camp than as a leader. There was one Stalin, but millions of victims.

These ideologies tend to overlook the fact that people differ from one another, with varying needs and desires. They fail to take into account that society is made up not only of two classes – the oppressors and the oppressed – but of a multitude of people, groups and subgroups. The dynamics of wealth and poverty are fluid, not static: most people repeatedly move up and down the economic ladder throughout their lives. Moreover, humans are social creatures – when they observe someone receiving the same money as themselves, but without working for it, they too may stop working. When we recognize that hard work leads to rewards and that individuals can advance their status, we can engage in healthy competition for limited resources, thereby generating wealth and increasing happiness.

THERE IS NO REALITY

Rob had just bought a stunning new convertible. He had picked it up from the agency and proudly parked it next to the high rise building where he lived. The next day was to be an eventful day at his office, with an annual gathering in the parking lot where colleagues would seize the opportunity to showcase their prized vehicles. Many of his friends were classic car enthusiasts, and Rob had been driving a well-maintained but old BMW. He planned to showcase his dazzling new sky-blue convertible the following day. He had been imagining how he would park it where everyone could see it. For a few weeks now, he had been flirting with a stunning girl from the neighbouring department who shared his passion for cars and drove a sleek, vintage grey Mustang. During a recent conversation, he had mentioned his new pride and joy, and she had made him promise to let her take it for a spin. Hearing she would be the first one to drive it, she had smiled and winked, this making her baby face and long blonde hair look even sexier.

The following morning Rob woke up early, put on his best suit, polished his shoes and sprayed on his best perfume. He took the lift down, eager to see his car. It was parked where he had left it – but it was damaged. The entire right side was wrecked. Another car had obviously smashed into his new pride and joy. Engine oil and radiator fluid, covered the ground. However, the driver's door was undamaged. Rob got into the car and tried to start the engine. He kept trying, thinking of how he would impress everyone with this beautiful car. He refused to accept the car was damaged. He did not want to think about repairs or assessments. It might be OK after all, he reasoned, or it might just be in his head.

A crowd gathered, and the police arrived on the scene. A policeman told him he needed to move the vehicle, as it could not remain parked there. The officer seemed upset by scene of the damage and suggested Rob get the car towed away to a workshop to be fixed and offered to help. Rob responded with a smile, insisting to the officer that, despite appearances, the car was fully functional. 'If it appears damaged to you, it's just fine by me,' he asserted confidently. 'It will run, and I'll drive it to work. My future wife is waiting to see it. She'll take it for a spin, and then I'll ask her out. Our first kiss will be in this car.'

'This car is gone,' the policeman told him.

'This is your perception,' Rob replied.

'No, this is the reality.'

'There is no such thing as the reality. What you see as reality is only your own subjective understanding, which is biased by default. I have my reality – I think the car is fine. It was parked where I left it and, logically, no one could have hit it; if they had, they would have left a note or attempted to contact me. I live in this building and they could have spoken with the concierge. Also, no one saw any accident, so there's no way it happened. I parked the car 10 hours ago, and the street is usually empty at that time. So, again, an accident here is highly unlikely.'

The policeman called for the paramedics, suggesting they take Rob to a psychiatric institution. Rob resisted, insisting he could not afford to be late. In the end, he was taken to a mental hospital against his will. While there, he argued with the doctors, asserting his own sanity and suggesting they were the ones who needed treatment.

'This is my understanding,' he told them. 'Reality is subjective, and hence you must respect my perspective. You need to understand that your institution and your discipline represent a power structure. By labelling people as insane, you are controlling and abusing humans. This practice must be cancelled.'

Many individuals reason similarly to Rob when faced with challenges. Have you met the morbidly obese, unemployed girl who believes she will land a well-paying job in a successful company, and become slim and popular without a real actionable plan? Or the 40-year-old man who spends his days playing computer games but thinks he is successful, attractive and on his way to becoming a great leader? This type of thinking – being preoccupied with abstract dreams – obstructs us from achieving our goals. More importantly, people's lack of awareness about their situation and environment is a significant barrier to a good life. As long as they are unable to grasp reality, distorting it with wishful thinking, they will not achieve much. Sooner or later, dreamers wake up to reality, which can cause all kinds of psychological problems.

This pattern of thinking, where individuals live in denial of their reality and construct elaborate fantasies, can be detrimental to them. It often results in a lack of progress because fantasists do not address real issues. Instead, they may continue to live in a bubble, avoiding the dedication and hard work required to achieve true success and happiness. Such a mindset may lead to serious mental health issues, including anxiety and depression, once reality sets in and the individual's dreams collapse.

In essence, the disconnect between one's perception and reality may cause significant cognitive dissonance (conflict) – a state of mental discomfort that arises from holding two conflicting beliefs, values or attitudes at the same time. This dissonance can give rise to various psychological stressors and impede an individual's ability to make rational decisions and take actions that align with their actual circumstances and goals. Therefore, it is crucial for individuals to engage in self-reflection and reality-checking to align their aspirations with real-life situations and capabilities. This approach not only fosters genuine progress but also helps build resilience, paving the way to more substantial and lasting achievements.

Chapter 5.
Self-help books between science and opium

Most people do not really want freedom, because freedom involves responsibility, and most people are frightened of responsibility.

Freud, 1930

THE SUPERPOWER WITHIN YOU

'I have been trying to awaken the giant within me for decades with no success. I have done everything in the book and truly believed in myself but, unfortunately, nothing happened.' Then he continued, saying: 'I think the giant within me must be dead by now.'

This is how I was introduced to Tony Robbins's book *Awaken the Giant Within* many years ago when an inpatient in a rehab centre was describing his efforts to deal with his various psychological issues over the years. At that time, I had never heard of that book. Like with the other self-help books I discuss here, it was mainly patients who made me aware that millions of people rely on such literature to deal with their psychological issues, to make sense of themselves, this world and others around them.

These well-advertised books are widely available, while the books we study and teach in psychology and psychiatry are off the radar for most people. A striking thing I have found is the number of patients who assume that, as a psychologist, I must be familiar with these bestsellers.

The plot of *Awaken the Giant Within* is well established, simple, attractive and yet could be harmful. We all suffer and dream of attaining grand goals, changing ourselves, the world, and influencing other people. Most of us, evidently, have failed so far in doing that. But Tony Robbins is an exception. He achieved his grand dream despite the giant obstacles he faced. He transformed himself from being a poor janitor into someone who now owns a helicopter and a '400-square-foot bachelor apartment in Venice'. Thousands of people who follow him travel to listen to his motivational talks. They are deeply grateful for his ideas, as he has helped them immensely. He has changed not only his own life but also the lives of many thousands of others, and this is why they cannot stop thanking him and appreciating his ingenuity. He has discovered the hidden secret to success and is happy to share it with whoever buys his books and pays to attend his talks.

On the first page of his book, Robbins tells his readers that his book transformed a child from being labelled 'hyperactive' and 'learning disabled' into being 'evaluated at the level of genius'. He also says a man told him how he freed himself from cocaine through using Robbins's techniques. He assures his ideas made a destitute guy very rich, fixed a broken marriage and made a woman lose 'fifty-two pounds'.

Awaken the Giant Within is based on the old theme that suffering humans need a saviour, who in this case happens to be Tony Robbins. He himself used to suffer greatly, but then discovered the solution and changed his life. If you want to change your life, buy Robbins's book, attend his talks and believe in him.

This is enticing, much like a Ponzi scheme, as it activates the human desire for discovering hidden secrets and quick fixes. Similar to a Ponzi scheme, Robbins's approach promises high returns (personal transformation and enormous success) with minimal effort, which is a hallmark of such schemes. While most would realise this is too good to be true or that these grand claims lack sufficient evidence, some people would take the risk, especially since the book is not that expensive. So why not give it a try? If it does not work, it will not harm, will it?

The devil is in the details

When Robbins explains how people can change their lives as he says he did, he starts by telling his readers to 'Raise Your Standards'. He claims that the same power available to Leonardo da Vinci, Abraham Lincoln, Helen Keller, Mahatma Gandhi, Einstein and others 'is available to you'. This absurd claim shows an inability to understand the complexity, diversity and richness of human nature.

The idea that everyone has the same genetic makeup, social and financial conditions, and hence anyone can be a Da Vinci, is an illogical myth that gives listeners a false hope that leads to despair. Each person mentioned as an 'inspiring example' is a product of his or her unique genes, culture, point in history, abilities and decisions. Da Vinci was a polymath who studied with great painters, sculptors, engineers and scholars. He grew up in a city teeming with art, wealth and culture. If he had been born in a remote, poor village in Sweden or Latvia, he might not have found someone to teach him to paint, let alone patrons such as the Medicis to finance his work or a pope to buy his paintings. Da Vinci was an exceptional person with an exceptional abilities who was born in the right time and ate the right place. There are probably people who could outperform da Vinci but for sure it is not the case for all of us or the majority.

Similarly, Abraham Lincoln was an elected president and a member of a political party. Whatever success he achieved in war or politics resulted from a multitude of factors, not merely because he raised his standards or believed in himself. It is nonsense to suggest that merely raising one's standards can replicate such historical feats. It ignores the complex interplay of multiple factors that led to success. Also, the individuals Robbins describes as 'inspiring examples' may not be seen as such by the vast majority of people. Few want to have blood on their hands like Lincoln or end up lonely like Einstein or spend their days working hard like Da Vinci.

Furthermore, the notion of raising one's standards is nothing but a vague concept, at best. Robbins alleges that if people tell themselves they will not accept less than what they want and will aim for more, it will motivate them to achieve whatever they desire. But could such a notion withstand rigorous testing? Could Robbins conduct a study to examine how many of those who read his books or attended his workshop have seen significant improvement in their conditions and how long that improvement lasted? What percentage of people followed his instructions yet found themselves worse off due to his ideas?

Rather than guaranteeing that anyone who reads the book or attends a specific number of workshops will attain his or her goals, Robbins includes a condition for success: sincere belief. He states, 'If you raise the standards but you don't really believe you can meet them, you've already sabotaged yourself'. This condition shifts the burden of proof to the followers rather than Robbins. If you succeeded, it's because you believed in the techniques; if you didn't, it's because you didn't sincerely believe. How can one judge sincere belief from a superficial one?

Throughout his 497-page book, Tony Robbins keeps repeating the same idea – that a person can achieve anything. He uses phrases such as 'Harness the Power of Decision', 'Live by the Principle of CANI' and other similar vague notions. Robbins keeps creating rules and formulas for people to follow to be as successful as he is. These are meant to change everything for the person. Through this endless repetition, he creates what is called the illusory truth effect. People tend to believe what has been repeated, even if it is irrational.

People who believe the notion that they can achieve anything and change their behaviour and way of thinking just by repeating phrases to themselves would most likely suffer great disappointment when they realise they have failed. Even worse, when they are told other people have succeeded while they have not, they tend to blame themselves for failing. This makes them less likely to try again or look for the reasons why they failed.

One of the ideas that I find particularly dangerous is that a self-help book can free someone from addiction. Addiction is one of the most harmful and difficult mental disorders to deal with. It has a multitude of underlying causes and needs to be treated in accordance with a scientific medical approach. Telling people that someone read a book or attended a workshop or a talk and healed from addiction can lead to extremely dangerous consequences. If recovering from cocaine addiction were that easy, rehab centres and mental institutions would have closed, and we would have saved billions of dollars and millions of lives. The same goes for dietitians, gyms and marriage counsellors. In fact, why not teach self-help books instead of science in high schools!

If we used the scientific method to understand the world, we would find that the odds of people recovering from addiction on their own without professional help are extremely low, even though a few might have done it. Moreover, stopping drug use can lead to severe withdrawal symptoms that might include life-threatening conditions. This is why medical supervision is crucial during detoxification process to ensure safety and provide appropriate treatments to alleviate symptoms.

Some people survive a bullet to the head, but most do not. Rational people do all they can to avoid such a death.

IMMUNE TO TRUTH

A man with a conviction is a hard man to change. Tell him you disagree and he turns away. Show him facts or figures and he questions your sources. Appeal to logic and he fails to see your point.
Leon Festinger, 1956

Uri Geller's book *My Story: The Bendest of the Spoon-Benders* and Tony Robbins's *Awaken the Giant Within* share similar themes. Geller's ideas and performances, while popular for years, need no deep analysis here. The most interesting part of Geller's story is how people continued to believe in him despite overwhelming evidence of his fraudulent claims.

Geller claimed to possess extraordinary psychic powers. These included telekinesis (being able to move objects without touching them), telepathy (reading other people's thoughts) and the power to bend metal objects, especially spoons, with his mind. He carried out these feats on television shows and in live performances, quickly gaining fame in the 1970s. Geller's demonstrations captivated audiences worldwide, leading to his appearing many times on television and getting massive media coverage.

Geller's fame extended beyond the general public, for he also garnered the support of notable figures. Among his fans were scientists such as dr Andrija Puharich, who conducted research on Geller's abilities; professor John Taylor, who at first gave Geller good reviews before concluding he did not possess any supernatural abilities after all; and astronaut Edgar Mitchell, who believed in Geller's psychic powers. Celebrities and public figures, including John Lennon, were initially fascinated by Geller's abilities.

The television exposure that should have ended it all

In 1973, Geller appeared on 'The Tonight Show Starring Johnny Carson'. Carson, a former magician himself, was sceptical of Geller's claims. He prepared a controlled environment with the help of magician and sceptic James

Randi to prevent Geller from performing any trickery. Under these conditions, Geller failed to perform his usual psychic feats, struggling to demonstrate his abilities on live television. Geller thought he was finished after being exposed, yet, surprisingly, the show made many new people believe in him.

James Randi's exposure

James Randi, a renowned magician and sceptic, was one of Geller's most outspoken critics. In his 1982 book *The Truth About Uri Geller*, Randi details how Geller's tricks can be replicated by using simple sleight-of-hand techniques and other forms of deception. Randi's thorough documentation and analysis, with clear evidence and logic, took apart Geller's claims of supernatural abilities.

Geller's continuing influence and wealth

Despite being exposed, Uri Geller has continued to enjoy considerable support. Also, his appearances, books and endorsements have brought him huge wealth. Geller capitalised on his fame by branching out into various ventures, including consulting for mining companies, where he claimed to use his dowsing abilities to locate mineral deposits. It is estimated Geller has amassed millions of dollars over his career.

Geller has remained a popular figure on television and in the wider media, leveraging his fame to maintain his public profile. Despite the controversies surrounding his abilities, he has cultivated relationships with influential individuals who have continued to support and believe in him.

WHY DO THEY REJECT THE FACTS?

The persistent belief in discredited figures and ideas can be explained by various psychological theories, including external attribution for negative outcomes and cognitive dissonance theory. Cognitive dissonance theory suggests that people strive for internal consistency. When faced with two or more ideas that contradict each other, individuals experience discomfort and often reject or rationalise the conflicting evidence so they can maintain their beliefs.

People who believe in the superpowers of a person or entity often internalize these beliefs, making them difficult to reject even when proven false. This is similar to a man who, after 25 years of a happy marriage, discovers that his loving and committed wife is currently having multiple affairs and has had many throughout their marriage. There is a high probability he will reject the evidence to maintain his belief, as acknowledging the truth would disrupt his long-held perceptions, emotional stability, and self-image.

In Geller's case, many have invested emotionally and mentally in his supposed abilities. They have normalised, internalised and justified his irrational ideas. Accepting the truth about his supposed powers would cause them major discomfort. Instead, they simply keep believing. Additionally, those who accept the illusion of Geller's psychic abilities prefer to see themselves as intelligent rather than as deceived.

What is more, some people enjoy being controversial and standing out. For example, when the majority asserts, based on facts, that the Earth is a sphere, they argue it's a flat disk, relishing the attention they receive for their odd views.

Islamic investment companies in Egypt

A good example of how people can be immune to facts on a large scale is the case of Islamic investment companies in Egypt in the 1980s. In the late 1970s and early 1980s, Egypt witnessed a rise in Islamic sentiment, and many Islamic investment companies were established. These firms appealed to devout Muslims by offering investments that adhered to Islamic law (Sharia), which does not allow the earning of interest on loans. Promising returns much higher than the banks, they attracted millions of Egyptians eager to invest their savings in what they believed was both profitable and halal.

These companies, claiming to invest in sectors such as real estate, manufacturing, and agriculture, amassed billions of Egyptian pounds, and people were competing to invest with them. They offered different types of investment plans with some guaranteeing over 100 per cent annual profit.

However, by the mid-1980s, it became clear these companies were Ponzi schemes. They paid returns to earlier investors using the money from new investors rather than profits from business activities. The schemes began to collapse when they could no longer attract enough new investors to pay the promised returns, and people began demanding their money back.

The collapse of these investment companies led to widespread financial ruin. Many Egyptians lost their life savings, and the country's economy was devastated. The government intervened, shutting down these companies and prosecuting some of the fraudsters. Several high-profile figures were jailed, while others fled the country.

Despite this, some of the fraudsters retained a high level of respect and followers. Many people, even those who lost their savings, continued to believe in the fraudsters' integrity. They attributed the downfall to conspiracies by the government or foreign entities rather than acknowledging the fraudulent nature of the schemes. To this day, many deny they were fools to part with their life savings while believing uneducated young men could outperform banks and well-established financial institutions. In a recent conversation on X (formerly Twitter) between one of the known fraudsters and people who lost their savings, the fraudster admitted the whole thing was a scam from the get-go and asked to be forgiven. Most refused to believe him or blame themselves for trusting such a charlatan. Some blamed the government for intimidating him, while others blamed it for not regulating him when he started.

This case shows how deeply ingrained beliefs, the tendency to blame others for one's mistakes, and the desire to justify personal or social values can lead people to reject logic and fact. Even when faced with overwhelming evidence, the temporary psychological comfort of maintaining one's beliefs and a positive self-image, coupled with the urge to avoid the pain of accepting harsh truths, may outweigh the desire to remain true to oneself and see the world as it is.

WHO ARE YOU?

Jen Sincero's bestselling book *You Are a Badass: How to Stop Doubting Your Greatness and Start Living an Awesome Life* starts with a story of her life-changing experience at

Halloween that happened when she was 2 years old. She explains how she was scared and forced to say, 'Trick or treat', but the sweets she got from the first house transformed her from a shy, frightened child into a loud, ambitious person who eagerly went from door to door screaming, 'Trick or treat!' – at the age of 2.

Sincero also remembers her costume exactly and describes it in detail. This story is designed to present her as someone special, almost holy: she still remembers what happened in detail when she was 2 years old. Unlike most humans, she does not suffer from childhood amnesia.

She then shares her motivation and credentials for writing a self-help book:

> My story of going from being forty, broke, and living in a converted garage in an alley to using spiritual concepts to get over my money hang-ups and finally make a whole bunch of it inspired me to write this book; but it's the countless emails and videos and letters that I have received from people over the past decade that have kept me inspired, kept me walking my talk, suiting up in my writing uniform (known to some as a bathrobe) year after year, and sitting down to write the next *Badass* book. (p.2)

Here again, Sincero portrays herself as a grand character who managed to turn her life around from one extreme to another. She presents herself as a selfless person writing this book to help others who keep contacting her, continually asking for her wisdom. She goes on to explain how many people have benefited from her book:

> I've heard from countless people who've used what they learned from it to manifest the things and experiences

they put on their vision boards with hair-raising accuracy (flying on the same private jet in the photo, buying the exact house they cut out, walking down the same beach they pictured with their soul mate). I've heard from a woman who went from being on food stamps for eight years to making seven figures after fully understanding that she was not a victim of circumstances but rather could create whatever she wanted. (p. 2)

Throughout the book, Sincero asserts that focusing on positive outcomes can turn those notions into reality: 'What you focus on you create more of in your life (p. 180); 'What you focus on, you create more of, and if you keep expecting people to annoy you they will not let you down' (p.128); 'What you choose to focus on becomes your reality' (p. 137).

However, the law of attraction, a concept Sincero heavily promotes, is rooted in pseudo-science – it lacks any proof and creates mythical individuals. The idea that thoughts alone can directly change the external world flies in the face of principles of science, logic and fact.

The book's most harmful aspect is its promotion of mythical thinking. Sincero frequently makes statements that suggest a magical view of the world, such as her assertion 'The Universe will match whatever vibration you put out. You can't fool The Universe' (p. 32). Or 'The decision to put "Love yourself" at the end of every chapter was not made by me but rather was insisted upon by the force that delivers thoughts to our minds and words to the page' (p. 9).

This type of thinking – which implies that the universe responds to individual vibrations, and a superpower helped her write the book – reflects irrational beliefs that mislead readers into believing their thoughts alone can shape reality. These ideas can be very harmful, as they lead individuals to ignore practical actions and real-world constraints, potentially resulting in disappointment, self-doubt and disillusionment when their expectations fail to happen.

IT'S A SECRET

The Secret, authored by Rhonda Byrne in 2006, is another best-selling book promoting harmful mythical thinking. I was introduced to this book by several patients who were surprised that I didn't read the 'important book'. Similar to *Badass*, the book is based on pseudo-science, misrepresentation of scientific principles and oversimplification of complex psychological and social phenomena.

The Secret tells people they are not living the life they should because they either do not know the magical rule of the law of attraction or, worse, are using it in the wrong way. After building up the negativity of our lives, Byrne gives us the magical solution. She claims that all we need to attract happiness, health, wealth and success is to focus on these issues.

Byrne states, 'You are the most powerful magnet in the Universe. You contain a magnetic power within you that is more powerful than anything in the world, and this unfathomable magnetic power is emitted through your thoughts' (p. 9). She also asserts, 'Your thoughts are the primary cause of everything' (p. 16). And, 'You are the one who calls the law of attraction into action, and you do it through your thoughts' (p. 35).

The influence of such irrational thinking is not only scientifically unfounded but can also hinder people's personal development. Believing that thoughts alone can change external reality can discourage people from taking action to achieve their goals. For example, someone who believes visualizing success is enough to succeed may neglect the hard work, planning and perseverance needed to maintain sufficient income. This mindset can create a false sense of security and result in agony, which ultimately hinders personal and professional prospects.

Byrne dangerously oversimplifies complex psychological issues. She often offers advice that, while motivational, lacks depth and fails to acknowledge the hurdles involved in overcoming personal challenges. For example, she advises readers to 'decide you want it more than you're afraid of it'. This statement, though encouraging, does not address the many-sided nature of fear, hope, personality traits (characteristics) and motivation. Overcoming fear often requires more than a simple talk; it involves understanding the root causes of the fear, developing coping strategies and sometimes seeking professional help. Therapies use structured techniques and professional guidance to get to the root of a fear and judge if it is rational and healthy or irrational and harmful. Therapists work with clients to address ideas as well as their emotions and the effects of these. Within psychotherapy, it is common to discover that the client's fear is based on reason rather than distorted thinking patterns. Fear sometimes plays an important role in motivation as well as in preserving a person's life. Public speakers, actors and musicians, for example, experience high levels of anxiety that make them rehearse beforehand and do their utmost during a performance.

Furthermore, Byrne uses personal stories to illustrate her points, such as when she states, 'I know it sounds weird, but when I started loving myself, my life completely changed'. While these can be powerful and easy to relate to, they are not proof that her ideas are correct. Personal stories are limited because they cannot prove cause and effect or be generalized to larger groups. Scientific conclusions require systematic investigation, replication and peer review.

In addition to these critical points, it is important to consider the broader implications of promoting books that rely heavily on fallacies and irrational thinking. This genre of self-help that encourages people to believe in mythical ideas can influence a wide audience, and foster a culture of idleness and superstition.

UNLOCK YOUR POTENTIAL

One of the central planks of self-help literature is that people possess untapped potential that, once unlocked, can lead to great personal and professional achievements. It suggests we are all born as geniuses and, over time, our creativity and ability to learn grow less. However, this view is often built on lies and faulty logic.

Measuring creativity is complex, and even childhood tests, designed for widespread use among children, rarely accommodate this complexity. The idea of unlocking personal potential, where readers are encouraged to explore their abilities, cultivate new skills and push beyond perceived limitations, is often intertwined with the notion of self-discovery and empowerment. Yet, it is crucial to recognise that many books in this genre propagate myths, such as the notion that we use only a small part of our brains. Or that the mind is distinct from the brain, our brains are split into separate parts and humans have superpowers or a sixth sense.

If you want to jam your brain, lose a significant number of neurons, and be left confused, go ahead and believe *Atomic Habits*. James Clear's book – which has sold 8 million copies – is a good example of how attractive mythical solutions are.

Clear begins with a story about the transformation of British Cycling:

> The fate of British Cycling changed one day in 2003. The organization, which was the governing body for professional cycling in Great Britain, had recently hired Dave Brailsford as its new performance director. At the time, professional cycling in Great Britain had endured nearly one hundred years of mediocrity. Since 1908, British riders had won just a single gold medal at the Olympic Games, and they had fared even worse in cycling's biggest race, the Tour de France. In 110 years, no British cyclist had ever won the event…
>
> Brailsford and his coaches began by making small adjustments. They redesigned the bike seats to make them more comfortable and rubbed alcohol on the tires for a better grip. They asked riders to wear electrically heated overshorts…
>
> Just five years after Brailsford took over, the British cycling team dominated the road and track cycling events

at the 2008 Olympics in Beijing, where they won an astounding 60 percent of the gold medals… (D)uring the ten-year span from 2006 to 2017, British cyclists won 178 world championships and sixty-six Olympic gold medals and captured five Tour de France victories. (p. 16)

From this account, we are led to believe Dave Brailsford single-handedly transformed British Cycling through minor adjustments, resulting in unparalleled success. However, the reality is more complex and less romantic.

The real story of British cycling

The change in fortunes of British Cycling began in 1997, not 2003, triggered by a substantial funding package from the British government, which allocated £40 million to various sports, including a significant amount specifically for cycling. In 1999, British Cycling secured additional lottery funding for six years, with the first year receiving £2.5 million.

This made British Cycling one of the best-funded teams in the world. That same year, the team won its first medal at a World Championship in 40 years. The lottery money enabled the acquisition of top-tier equipment, a vast support team and the recruitment and training of elite cyclists. By 2009, BSkyB began sponsoring the team with £15 million annually, further enhancing its competitive edge and enabling multiple Tour de France victories.

Contrary to Clear's narrative, the success was not due to a few minor adjustments by one intelligent individual but rather a huge financial overhaul. Thanks to this funding, British Cycling could afford top-notch equipment, an army of trainers, medical staff and cutting-edge training facilities, including the National Indoor BMX Centre, which alone cost £24 million in 2011. These major investments laid the foundation for success.

Dave Brailsford's philosophy of 'marginal gains' was built on an already solid base of prior financial backing. The idea was that by improving every aspect of cycling by just 1 per cent, the overall effect of these small gains would lead to significant performance improvements. These, which ranged from the more obvious, such as bike technology and training techniques, to the less conventional, such as optimising athletes' sleep environments and nutrition plans, would have been impossible without funding, infrastructure and management. Better performance resulted from this funding from the government, which in turn made the changes possible.

Misleading simplifications

Clear's narrative fits a popular idea in self-help literature: that small, simple changes can lead to massive success. While it is an appealing theory, it often overlooks the complexities and sidesteps facts and logic. In the case of British Cycling, success was due not merely to small tweaks – it also needed the extra money to support a world-class programme, along with strategic management and the cyclists' hard work. Recognising these facts is crucial to understanding why and how the team achieved success.

Clear also fails to mention the serious accusations of bullying, harassment and a culture of fear reported by several cyclists in the British Cycling team. The BBC aired a programme about these allegations, which included accusations of doping to improve performance. These controversies further disprove the story of simple, marginal gains leading to extraordinary success – the reality was a far more complex.

Clear presents the events in a way that perpetuates myths, persuading readers to accept these as truths.

False ideas and pseudo-expert knowledge

Like many other self-help books, *Atomic Habits* is written by someone who claims to understand the human psyche despite never having studied psychology, psychiatry, or sociology, never having worked in a mental health institution or conducted scientific research. The book assumes humans are the same as each other, and overlooks individual differences, varying personality traits, difference in IQ and the effect of circumstances. It argues we have automatic habits we need to control to succeed in life and reach our goals, despite the fact that each of us has different goals, abilities, perception and genetic makeup.

As we read further, we note that Clear does not define 'success' or 'automatic habits' scientifically. He does not specify whether he refers to our way of thinking, to perception, to reasoning patterns or to behaviours. Hence, throughout the book, we are left to guess what he means.

He makes numerous false, or rather farcical, claims about the human brain, contradicting both established scientific knowledge and logic. One such claim goes like this:

> In total, the framework I offer is an integrated model of the cognitive and behavioral sciences. I believe it is one of the first models of human behavior to accurately account for both the influence of external stimuli and internal emotions on our habits. (p. 14)

No! For any set of ideas to qualify as a model, it must be precise, based on objective, verifiable, and falsifiable data – criteria that Clear's descriptions do not satisfy. Rather, it is empty talk based on obsolete concepts, such as B.F. Skinner's 1930s reductionist understanding of human behaviour as the product of reward and punishment, which shows a complete lack of understanding of neuropsychology and cognitive psychology.

Clear also says, 'Human behavior is always changing: situation to situation, moment to moment, second to second. But this book is about what doesn't change. It's about fundamentals of human behavior. The lasting principles you can rely on year after year.' (p. 14). The first part of this false and self-contradictory statement opposes tens of thousands of studies in personality, cognitive, forensic and social psychology which have shown that human behaviour is not 'always changing' but is relatively consistent.

Clear also claims:

> The strategies I cover will be relevant to anyone looking for a step-by-step system for improvement, whether your goals center on health, money, productivity, relationships, or all of the above. As long as human behavior is involved, this book will be your guide. (p. 14)

From this statement, it seems there is almost nothing this book can't do. Who needs universities, research centres, experts, and conferences when we have this book? Clear has found the missing link: human behaviour is governed by a limited number of principles, and by controlling these, we can improve our lives and achieve our goals. This same misleading idea is often used by fortune tell-
ers, conspiracy theorists and fraudsters. They all claim

to have uncovered hidden truths, without the backing of laboratories, peer-reviewed papers, research teams or proof. Instead, they rely on passionate language and their personal assurances to convince others.

Repeating a 'behaviour' versus a 'habit'

Another fallacy in Clear's argument is illustrated by this statement:

> Habits are the compound interest of self-improvement. The same way that money multiplies through compound interest, the effects of your habits multiply as you repeat them. They seem to make little difference on any given day and yet the impact they deliver over the months and years can be enormous. It is only when looking back two, five, or perhaps ten years later that the value of good habits and the cost of bad ones becomes strikingly apparent. (p. 18)

This is an example of the failure to separate different types of behaviour and to understand how cognition, emotions and behaviour work together, as well as the notion of how we build thoughts. It is false to assume that simply repeating a behaviour will make it a habit. For a behaviour to be repeated consistently, there must be a reasoning and motivation, and sometimes a biological foundation, behind it.

For instance, consider drug addicts who stay for months in a rehabilitation centre or jail, where they are kept away from drugs and take part in healthy routines such as waking up every morning at the same time, eating nutritious food, exercising and reading. Upon release, many revert to drug use and abandon the healthy habits developed during their confinement.

What makes a person start using drugs in the first place? Most addicts abstain from substances for at least the first 17 years of their lives. So, why can they not continue resisting them, like most people? Because the motivations of people who become, and continue as, drug addicts differ from those of the greater part of society.

Another obvious example is our daily routine of waking up every morning to go to work or school. We break this habit during holidays or when work is cancelled due to weather conditions. Students do not go to school on Saturdays simply out of habit – their behaviour adjusts according to their circumstances.

A person's ideas guides their actions

Evidence-based psychotherapy is founded on the principle that human behaviour results from ideas, is justified by other ideas, and links to patterns of thinking. Even individuals with schizophrenia do not act without reason: their cultural and educational backgrounds tend to shape their delusions. For instance, educated schizophrenics are more likely to have delusions involving aliens and computers, while uneducated people who live in cultures that believe in spirits and black magic develop delusions related to these issues.

Education is based on building up a complex system of ideas and skills composed of many smaller applied parts. People who want to become medical doctors must learn chemistry, biology, maths and anatomy but, before all that, how to read and write. Then they need to understand germ theory and the definition of different illnesses, their symptoms and how to diagnose and stay up to date with various treatments, how well they work and side effects. To succeed, they must possess specific features, such as good memory, dedication, high intelligence and resilience.

To maintain any behaviour, people need justification. They abuse drugs to avoid stress, seek a thrill or cope with situations. Therefore, to create lasting change in behaviour, it is crucial first to examine and alter underlying ideas for each person rather than presenting a one-size-fits-all solution.

STOP WASTING YOUR MONEY ON CAFÉS

A client of mine was spending nearly a third of his income at coffee shops. He would start his day with a visit to his favourite Starbucks branch. Then, at noon, he had to go for a sandwich and another coffee and, after finishing work, would grab another coffee. In the evening, he enjoyed a caffeine-free hot drink with a small cake. Many had tried to convince him to stop this extravagant habit. He had been told time and again that the money spent on coffee should go towards his household. He would listen carefully, agree with them, and continue with his habit. He said he never sincerely intended to stop and had never been convinced by people's arguments. They failed to understand that this was part of his identity and coping strategy.

He was unhappy in his marriage, had issues with his two brothers who lived in the same building as him, had few friends and had grown up in poverty. He enjoyed meeting his friends and different people while sitting having his coffee and reading newspapers. For him, sitting in these cafés made him feel better about himself. There he could also avoid arguing with his wife and brothers. If he stayed at home, he was sure he would get a divorce, something neither he nor his wife could afford or wanted at the time. Hence, he spent his time in cafés, while she had the apartment to herself to entertain her friends. She enjoyed watching soap operas and eating, drinking and gossiping with her friends more than anything else, he said. He felt hurt whenever someone told him to make his own coffee and food and stop wasting money on coffee shops. 'They assume they know me better than I know myself. They insult my intelligence and interfere in my life.'

'Identity Emerges Out of Habits' – seriously?!?

In chapter 2 of *Atomic Habits*, titled 'How Your Habits Shape Your Identity (and Vice Versa)', the author states, 'Your identity emerges out of your habits. You are not born with pre-set beliefs. Every belief, including those about yourself, is learned and conditioned through experience' (p. 34). It is obvious that Clear has no idea about biological foundation of behaviour or what 'identity' is, or that there is something called 'collective identity'.

Collective identity relates to our affiliation with different groups such as a nation, religion and culture, and what that means for us. These affiliations can be so strong that people are willing to sacrifice their lives for them, despite not choosing to be born into them. Conversely, people may leave their home country, change their names, religions and language – yet their core identity remains influenced by their past and their experiences. Identity is one of the most complex notions in psychology, an arena of fierce debate among scientists, and reducing it to something that emerges from habits is highly misleading.

'The book helped me'

Why does *Atomic Habits* seem to work for some people? To take such a claim seriously, we would need to see the percentage of people who benefited from this book, the extent of their behavioural improvements and how long these lasted. How many goals did they achieve? When suggesting a psychological idea, it is crucial to demonstrate how effective it might be and potential side effects.

Countless people claim to have been helped by simple ideas from self-help books, life coaches and motivational talks. However, these effects have never been documented and are mostly exaggerated. Some people tend to believe that since they have put some effort into a task, they must have gained something. For instance, they may feel the bad relationships they went through made them better, stronger people. This idea may be true to some degree, but one can also argue that these people wasted valuable parts of their lives and endured unnecessary suffering. Moreover, bad relationships tend to leave stains on our self-image and distort our perspective, and we are better off without such experiences.

Furthermore, people who search for such books and read them are often ready to change, and this aids their perceived success. The question for anyone who claims *Atomic Habits* helped them is to show the extent to which and how long the effects of the change lasted and to consider other factors that might have contributed to the change.

The harm of a magic fix

Throughout his book, Clear fails time and again to grasp the complexity of human behaviour, making broad generalizations without objective evidence. Such books can be very harmful, as they promise a magical fix, leading people to blame themselves for failure rather than being realistic about their true abilities and limits.

Finally, would Clear be willing to test his model in a rehab centre, a forensic ward or an educational setting? Would any university or serious researcher design a study or therapy based on Clear's model?

SELF-CHANGE IS EASY

Have you managed to avoid coming across *The Subtle Art of Not Giving a F*ck* by Mark Manson? Another well-advertised yet harmful piece of nonsense, this book is rife with inaccuracies and baseless assertions. It lacks logical reasoning, contradicts facts and presents yet another mythical argument based on false ideas.

In the first chapter, we are given a fictional biography of Charles Bukowski, introduced as:

> an alcoholic, a womanizer, a chronic gambler, a lout, a cheap-skate, a deadbeat, and on his worst days, a poet. He is probably the last person on earth you would ever look to for life advice or expect to see in any sort of self-help book. Which is why he is the perfect place to start. Bukowski wanted to be a writer. But for decades his work

was rejected by almost every magazine, newspaper, journal, agent, and publisher he submitted to... (T)hirty
years went by like this, most of it a meaningless blur of
alcohol, drugs, gambling and prostitutes. Then, when Bukowski was fifty, after a lifetime of failure and self-loathing, an editor at a small independent publishing house
took a strange interest in him. (p. 1)

If you care to know the true story of Bukowski's life, here it
is. At the age of 24, Bukowski published a short story titled
'Aftermath of a Lengthy Rejection Slip' in *Story Magazine*.
Two years later, he published another story. He continued
to read and write throughout his life. Dissatisfied with the
publication processes, he paused his efforts to publish
for a time. However, by 1960, before his fortieth birthday,
he published three books, which are among his most significant works. Bukowski studied (albeit did not finish)
journalism at Los Angeles City College. Throughout his life,
he was highly self-reliant, holding numerous jobs. Notably,
he worked for the United States Postal Service for 12 years,
eventually leaving the job to focus on writing full-time after
receiving an offer from a publishing house.

Manson writes that Bukowski's success as a novelist and
poet defied everyone's expectations. Manson continues,
'despite the book sales and fame, Bukowski was a loser',
and claims Bukowski was successful due to being a failure:

See, despite the book sales and fame, Bukowski was a loser.
He knew it... He never tried to be anything other than
what he was. The genius in Bukowski's work was not in
overcoming unbelievable odds or developing himself into
a shining literary light. It was the opposite. It was his simple ability to be completely, unflinchingly honest with

himself – especially the worst parts of himself – and to share his failings without hesitation or doubt. This is the real story of Bukowski's success: his comfort with himself as a failure. Bukowski didn't give a fuck about success (p. 2, 3)

This is yet another narrative which implies that failure can turn into success with little or no effort. It suggests you can be a womaniser, alcoholic and loser all your life and suddenly become a success story. This alluring notion encourages passivity, leading people to believe they can achieve success and personal growth by doing nothing except wait for things to turn around on their own. Just think how damaging such ideas could be for young people.

Now losers can justify their laziness

Manson selectively uses Bukowski's writings, popular for various reasons, to pass a general judgement that Bukowski was a great, successful person and a role model from whom people must learn. Bukowski's history of womanising, which hurt many women, and his gambling addiction, which he openly acknowledged, are glossed over. Though he was a talented writer who pursued his passion, he neglected many important aspects of life. Significantly, Bukowski suffered physical and mental abuse as a child, which left a permanent mark on his self-perception and interactions with others.

Good is bad and bad is good?

Manson further writes, 'The desire for a more positive experience is itself a negative experience. And, paradoxically, the acceptance of one's negative experience is it-self a positive experience'. He continues to explain this illogical nonsense by rephrasing it as, 'wanting a positive experience is a negative experience; accepting a negative experience is a positive experience'.

So, according to Manson, the desire to care for one's children, help people in need, and support your mother can be seen as negative, while being an abusive parent, a lazy worker, and a narcissistic person is viewed as positive. Orwell must be laughing in his grave: 'War is peace and freedom is slavery!'

Your society is not your enemy

The book is riddled with contradictions and misconceptions, appealing to those who prefer to believe what they do not fully understand. On one hand, Manson argues individuals should live by values they think are important rather than those put forth by society. On the other hand, he argues that many values people desire are bad and should be dismissed. For example, he claims wanting to be popular is bad because it cannot be controlled, while values such as honesty and kindness are good because we can control them. He fails to notice that not everyone wants to be sociable and that kindness or honesty are subjective and related to society's values and norms. He separates what humans want as individuals from what society encourages. This contradictory notion defies logic and reality. Humans are integral to their cultures and societies. So, portraying society as an enemy forcing its members into adopting bad values is absurd.

Failing versus being a failure

The truth is, pursuing positive goals gives our lives meaning. The trouble is, some people do not know what their goals are. Each of us is different, and we need to accept that fact. We vary in our abilities, desires, emotions and ways of thinking. Therefore, we ought to have various goals and pursue them according to our capacity. The values and goals endorsed by all human societies, regardless of race, language and culture, are many and diverse. Achievements such as being an honourable person, a world-class swimmer, a master chess player, a good parent, a decent neighbour, an influential orator, a successful businessman, a skilled surgeon, a witty politician or an ingenious teacher require hard work and are universally appreciated.

It is OK to fail sometimes, but it is not OK to give up and become a failure. Normalizing the negative is a bottomless pit filled with misery and suffering. Working hard, setting goals, experiencing disappointments and excitement, and ultimately feeling satisfied with oneself is immensely rewarding.

THE WORLD IS A SMALL VILLAGE

In the 1990s, I visited a small town in Oman renowned for its association with folk medicine and black magic. The scene was striking: long queues of people waiting outside the old, crumbling houses of magicians who called themselves healers and claimed to have supernatural powers. Assistants stood by, organizing the crowd and asking about their needs and desires: 'I want to be cured of lung cancer,' 'I want my daughter to be healed from autism,' 'I want my daughter to marry a wealthy man,' 'I want to become a doctor,' 'I want my brother to divorce his wife,' and so on.

I could see that, while some people wholeheartedly believed in this lunacy, many others were doubtful. They kept asking the assistants if their bosses would deliver and how they knew it was true. The assistants would promise that they would get whatever they came for and recount stories of many people who had supposedly received all kinds of things after believing in the blessed healers.

'My daughter was disabled, and the holy man sitting behind this door healed her. Since then, I have been serving him so he can help other people,' one assistant was telling a woman who seemed unconvinced by the high fees they were charging. Despite their doubts, many people paid the fees and brought offerings, not out of genuine belief, but out of a sense of desperate hope. Some just left.

This experience often comes to mind when I consider the modern fascination with techniques such as Neuro-Linguistic Programming (NLP), mind mapping, homeopathy and other similar approaches. The people who resort to these methods remind me of those who sought out the healers. Just as those hopefuls in Oman paid for dubious services, millions in the West invest in astrology, believe in pseudo-science, reincarnation and fortune-telling. Despite the lack of scientific evidence supporting these beliefs and practices, the allure of a simple trick or a quick fix remains powerful.

The appeal of these methods lies in their grand promise of easy and rapid transformation. NLP, for example, claims to offer techniques that improve communication,   131 personal development and psychotherapy. Mind mapping, while possibly a useful tool for organizing thoughts and information, is often oversold as a revolutionary technique for learning and creativity.

Belief in these ideas point to the human desire for control and certainty in an unpredictable world. Just as the people in Oman turned to magicians to address their life challenges, many today seek simple solutions to complex problems. This pattern highlights the timeless aspect of human nature: the bent towards believing in and seeking magical or pseudo-scientific solutions when faced with uncertainty.

Chapter 6.
Understand yourself

All the world's a stage,
And all the men and women merely players:
They have their exits and their entrances;
And one man in his time plays many parts,
His acts being seven ages.

Shakespeare, *As You Like It*

THE 'SELF' IN PSYCHOLOGY

The 'self' in psychology can be defined, for the sake of clarity, as our understanding of who we are, a concept that is highly complex, multifaceted and dynamic. This includes our personalities, collective identities, individual identities, and attitudes. It is often viewed as something deeply buried, layered with misconceptions, unconscious conflicts, desires, drives, biases, irrational beliefs, and both positive and negative thought patterns.

A major question in psychology is whether our expressed behaviours and emotions truly reflect our core selves, or if they are merely performances, as Shakespeare suggested. How much of our true self do we reveal versus what is hidden behind social masks? What is the self?

Within psychology, there are several theories, school of thoughts and understandings of the self. George Herbert Mead argued that the self develops through social interaction. According to Mead, the self emerges from social experiences and communication with others, involving both the spontaneous, active 'I' and the internalized social expectations of the 'Me.' This means that our self-concept is shaped by our interactions with society and our internalised perceptions of these interactions.

Erving Goffman suggested our self is a performance, likening social interaction to a theatrical play where individuals manage their impressions to control how others see them. This idea introduces the concept of 'dramaturgy' and suggests that much of what we present to the world is carefully managed.

Henri Tajfel and John Turner explored how group membership impacts self-concept through their Social Identity Theory. They argue that our self is partly defined by our group memberships and social categories, which significantly influence our behaviour and attitudes towards in-group and out-group members. We tend to categorize people as part of our group (in-group members) or as part of different groups (out-group members). Our evaluations of people are biased by whether we perceive them as similar to us and part of our group, or different and thus, part of another group.

Discourse theorists, who investigate psychological topics through analysing people's talk, offer a different perspective on the self. They emphasise how identities and the self are constructed and negotiated through language and within context. According to these studies, the self can be seen as continually constructed and reconstructed entity through discourse (talk). This perspective highlights the fluid and dynamic nature of who we are, shaped by the contexts and interactions in which it is expressed. It suggests that identity can be seen as something we build with words as an end or a means to further ends. Speakers tend to create and assume identities in relation to social interactions rather than revealing their true identity or self. Whether these presented selves genuinely reflect what the speakers think of themselves or not is another question.

KEY QUESTIONS FOR SELF-REFLECTION

It is hard for any person to understand his- or herself completely, let alone express this understanding directly. However, a number of questions can help us improve our self-understanding.

Do I have a psychological disorder?

Before delving into self-exploration and self-improvement, it is crucial to address your own mental health. Reflect on your thoughts, feelings and behaviours. Symptoms such as ongoing sadness, anxiety, mood swings and mental pain may signal underlying issues. Other signs include irrational beliefs, how well you can control your impulses, relationship struggles, inability to enjoy life, self-hatred and low self-esteem. If you suspect you have a mental disorder, seeking professional help is the first step. Ignoring these signs is like continuing to drive with the check-oil light flashing – eventually, you will break down.

Am I traumatized?

Childhood trauma is a critical factor that must be addressed. Many people have experienced mental, physical, or sexual abuse, as well as neglect. Acknowledging the suffering and understanding that you were a victim is often essential for moving on. Many people overcome trauma without developing pathological reactions or negative thought patterns. Others suffer from trauma-related psychological problems or develop destructive coping mechanisms without showing symptoms of a mental illness. Unfortunately, some people blame themselves and ruminate in harmful ways. Having someone who listens without judgment or unsolicited advice is vital. Seeking professional help and being forthcoming about the trauma and its effects might be necessary if you think you have a psychological disorder.

Am I living in a healthy environment?

Our social environment consists of the people we interact with, the nature of our relationships, and the norms and laws that regulate our lives. Reflect on your relationships: Do you genuinely love your parents, partner, children, and yourself? Can you express yourself freely? Are specific experiences traumatising you? Is your environment harming you physically, mentally, or emotionally? Is it enabling you? Do you feel appreciated and understood?

A healthy environment includes authentic relationships based on mutual feelings, understanding, support, and safety. You should be able to be yourself without fear of unjust judgment and find opportunities for personal development. Numerous studies indicate that a supportive environment can greatly impact mental health outcomes. Ask yourself if you are in good company, or are you surrounded by emotional vampires who suck you dry? Your environment should be like a greenhouse, nurturing your growth, not a battlefield draining your energy.

Many people cannot make drastic changes to their social environment, so they need to assess what they can and cannot tolerate, for how long, and the price they are willing to pay. Consider the alternatives and develop a plan with specific steps. This plan should be adaptable and include alternative options. If the plan fails, it is normal to feel disappointed for a while. Allow yourself time to regroup before moving on, whether with a revised plan or after taking a break.

Do you know your needs?

First, it is important to distinguish between needs and desires, although many times they may overlap. When I am starving, I need to eat but may refuse to do so because I am on a hunger strike. If I eat, I will betray my fellow strikers. Hence, I may come up with various mental images and strategies to suppress my hunger. I have another need, which is to remain a member of the group on hunger strike, especially if I know that letting them down may have severe consequences.

I need clothes for protection, but may desire to attract the attention of good-looking girls by wearing flashy outfits I cannot really afford. Similarly, I may want a specific car, clothes, or particular knowledge I do not actually need.

Understanding your needs is fundamental to self-awareness. Needs can change over time and vary from person to person. Ask yourself why you consider certain things to be basic needs and whether you have the means to fulfil them. Think of your needs as the foundation of a house—without a strong foundation, the entire structure is shaky. So, reflect deeply: Are these needs genuine, or are they influenced by society's expectations?

Do you have goals? What are they?
What does reaching these goals entail?
Do you have a way to achieve your goals?
Do you have a strategy to remain focused?

Setting goals is a crucial aspect of self-understanding and leading a meaningful life. Reflect on whether you have specific goals and the steps needed to achieve them. Goals provide direction and purpose, contributing to a sense of fulfilment and progress. Many studies emphasize the importance of goal-setting in enhancing motivation and performance. Imagine your goals as the GPS for your life's journey. You need to keep updating and adjusting the destination. Without goals, you are just driving around aimlessly, hoping to stumble upon something interesting. What are your goals, and do you have a roadmap to achieve them?

Happiness is a personal evaluation and feeling based on reality. It is related to achieving a purpose in your life that motivates you to invest in yourself and achieve a better understanding of who you are. Being aware of your weaknesses and desires helps you manage stress better and overcome life's challenges. Having children, being in love, pursuing a career, engaging in hobbies and belonging to a social group all give life meaning.

Do you have hopes?

> *To live without hope is to cease to live.*
> Dostoevsky

Hope is the fuel that keeps us going, even when the road gets bumpy. Consider what you hope for in life and how these aspirations shape your actions and mindset. Snyder's Hope Theory suggests that hope involves both the motivation to achieve goals and the perceived ways to reach them.

Hope is not wishful thinking or daydreams. While indulging in wishful thinking may give temporary relief, especially in reacting to a specific situation, it can cause extreme harm if it becomes a pattern. For instance, if you are insulted by the police while in a country with no real justice system, daydreaming of justice may be productive. It will allow you to restrain yourself from taking the law into your own hands and destroying your life. Usually people realise the reality of a situation and find a way to deal with it, such as emigrating from a country, establishing a connection elsewhere that will protect them from abuse, and so on. In some cases, however, daydreaming and wishful thinking that justice will be served and that the situation will be fixed on its own will only prolong the person's suffering. In that situation, they impede progress and conceal the reality.

Are You Flexible?

A proportion of relationships that began with love at first sight, blossomed into deep commitment, and led to marriage and children, ultimately end in family courts. We lose people we love and meet new people we come to love. Life is like an ongoing party where guests come and go until we ourselves leave. And the party continues.

Our social world is in a constant flow. We form relationships – some lasting a short time, some for decades, and some for life. Relationships can form due to proximity, shared interests, or coincidence. Some are positive, others negative.

The world itself is constantly changing. Two years ago, Ukraine and Israel were peaceful countries; today, they are war zones. In 1991, Kuwait was occupied by Iraqi soldiers, but a year later, it was prosperous and safe. After World War II, it took the Germans only a few years to rebuild their devastated country.

On a personal level, our cognitive and physical abilities, desires, needs change with age and experience. Tasks that were once easy become hard, and what was complex may become routine. We may like what we used to hate and detest what we used to admire.

'Flexibility' – was the answer of one of my mentors when I asked what made him successful. People who recognize the dynamic nature of themselves, the world and others can adapt better, are more likely to succeed, and live satisfying lives.

Ask yourself how flexible you are. What are the things you are willing to change? What are the things you want to change but cannot? And what are the things you can change but don't want to? Reflect on these questions.

Understanding yourself is an ongoing journey that involves asking the right questions and being honest with your answers. By exploring your mental health, addressing trauma, evaluating your environment, recognizing your needs, setting clear goals and fostering hope, you pave the way for a more fulfilling and meaningful life. Reflect regularly, adapt as necessary and always strive for self-improvement.

Chapter 7.
Understanding others

HOW CAN I CHANGE HER (HIM)?

Every semester, I give a talk about psychopathy and Cluster B personality disorders. One key thing people should learn about mental health is the nature and impact of these disorders. When I see how people suffer due to a lack of awareness, I feel like Ignaz Semmelweis, who urged people to wash their hands and not to trust doctors after he discovered many deaths were caused by unhygienic conditions during medical procedures. (That was mid-1840s.) I urge people to read about personality disorders, trust medical professionals and avoid toxic relationships. It's crucial to stress that these disorders can only be diagnosed by mental health professionals in a proper setting. You shouldn't label people or yourself without a professional diagnosis.

The notion that some people have odd characters resistant to change is as old as humanity. The Greek philosopher Theophrastus, who documented different types of people, used the term 'Unscrupulous Man' to describe what we today call psychopaths, those with antisocial personality disorder, and sociopaths. He lamented that such a person would deceive, steal, break the law, harm other people, and feel happy rather than guilty. Every time I discuss psychopathy, someone inevitably raises their hand to ask how to help these people, often revealing that they are in a relationship with someone exhibiting these symptoms. 'How can I change her/him?', they would ask.

Individuals with these disorders greatly benefit from recognising and addressing their conditions. More importantly, people with personality disorders significantly impact those around them and can pose serious dangers to themselves and others. Therefore, it is vital for everyone, not just those with personality disorders, to understand these conditions and know how to deal with the individuals who have them. Unlike mood disorders, which occur at specific times in one's life and often go into remission either on their own or with medication, personality disorders are more stable and persistent.

According to the DSM-5, 'A personality disorder is an enduring pattern of inner experience and behaviour that deviates markedly from the expectations of the individual's culture, is pervasive and inflexible, has an onset in adolescence or early adulthood, is stable over time, and leads to distress or impairment.' People with personality disorders perceive themselves, the world and others in ways that differ from what is considered normal within their cultures, causing distress to themselves and potential harm to others.

There are 10 recognised personality disorders, categorised into three main clusters: A, B, and C.

CLUSTER A: THE ECCENTRIC

Cluster A personality disorders are marked by behaviours and thought patterns that are particularly odd or eccentric, significantly deviating from societal norms. Individuals with these disorders often seem peculiar or socially detached, making it considerably difficult for them to form and maintain relationships. They tend not to trust other people and often prefer isolation. Their perceptions and interpretations of reality are frequently distorted, causing others to view these individuals as strange or bizarre. Consequently, they face significant social and work-related challenges, as their unusual behaviours and tendency to misinterpret others' actions impede normal functioning.

People with Cluster A personality disorders often struggle with social life. They tend to avoid close relationships and prefer solitary activities. Their emotional expression is often limited, making it hard for others to read their feelings or intentions. This detachment can be perceived as aloofness or indifference, further complicating their social interactions. The mistrust they feel towards others is deep-seated and pervasive, often leading them to interpret benign actions as malicious. This constant suspicion can make social and occupational environments feel threatening, pushing them further into isolation.

Individuals with these disorders may exhibit peculiar behaviours and thinking. They might hold odd beliefs or engage in magical thinking, believing in things that are generally considered irrational by societal standards. Their talk may be vague or overly elaborate, and their thought processes can be disorganised. Their appearance and gestures might also be unusual, which can be off-putting or confusing to others.

The social and occupational impairments faced by individuals with Cluster A disorders are significant. Their difficulty in forming and maintaining relationships can lead to a lack of social support, which is crucial for mental and emotional well-being. At work, their distrustful nature and poor interpersonal skills can create conflicts and misunderstandings, often putting their jobs at risk. Their strange behaviour and thinking can also hinder their ability to adapt to new situations or environments, limiting their opportunities for personal and professional growth.

Due to their mistrust, people with Cluster A disorders often avoid seeking help or being open about their problems. This avoidance can lead to a lack of diagnosis and treatment, worsening their symptoms and impairments. Even when they do seek help, their odd behaviours and ways of thinking can make it challenging for therapists to establish a rapport. The chronic nature of these disorders means that individuals might struggle with these issues throughout their lives, leading to lasting social isolation and occupational difficulties.

CLUSTER B: NEVER-ENDING WAR

Cluster B personality disorders are characterized by dramatic, intensely emotional, or erratic behaviour and thinking. Individuals with these disorders often experience unstable and volatile emotions, leading to turbulent relationships and impulsive actions. Their behaviour is unpredictable, and they are highly sensitive to criticism.

This cluster includes individuals who may lack empathy, crave constant admiration, and behave in manipulative and deceitful ways. Because of their extreme emotional responses, tendency to see relationships in black-and-white terms, as well as being prone to boredom, they find it challenging to maintain stable relationships.

People with Cluster B personality disorders often struggle with self-image and identity. Their sense of self can be highly unstable, shifting between feelings of grandiosity and deep insecurity. This instability often drives their dramatic behaviour and emotional outbursts. Their intense fear of abandonment can drive them to use desperate or manipulative tactics to keep relationships, however, their actions often have the opposite effect, pushing people away and creating a cycle of conflict and instability.

Initially, individuals with Cluster B disorders may come across as charming and charismatic. However, their manipulative tendencies can soon surface, causing trust issues and conflicts. Strong need for admiration and validation can lead to attention-seeking behaviours, which may be perceived as inappropriate or excessive. Their emotional reactions are often disproportionate to the situation, causing them to react with intense anger, sadness, or anxiety to minor provocations.

Their relationships often suffer the most, as the turbulent and unpredictable environment affects their partners, friends, and family members. They may oscillate between idealizing and devaluing others. The instability can result in frequent conflicts, breakups, and a lack of long-term support networks. Their relationships are often marked by intense, short-lived connections that burn out quickly.

Professionally, their impulsivity and interpersonal challenges can create a rocky career path. Conflicts with colleagues and superiors often lead to job losses or changes. Additionally, their impulsivity may result in poor decisions and risky behaviours. Their constant need for validation can also negatively impact their work performance, as they may focus more on seeking attention than on fulfilling their responsibilities.

CLUSTER C: THE ANXIOUS SHADOWS

Cluster C personality disorders are defined by pervasive anxiety and fearfulness. People with these disorders are often extremely self-conscious and sensitive to criticism and rejection. They are frequently overwhelmed by fear of social interactions, appearing shy or timid, and may go to great lengths to avoid situations where they might be judged or evaluated. This typically has a significant impact on their social and professional lives.

Socially, they often feel anxious and may avoid situations altogether or approach them with extreme caution and self-consciousness. This can lead to social isolation and a lack of meaningful relationships. Their fear of criticism and rejection makes them overly agreeable and submissive, often at the expense of their own needs and desires. They rely heavily on others for approval and reassurance, often displaying submissive and clinging behaviour. Such behaviours can lead to resentment and frustration, both for themselves and those around them.

In the workplace, individuals with Cluster C disorders may struggle with assertiveness and decision-making. They might avoid taking initiative and responsibility or expressing opinions, instead relying on others for guidance and approval. This behaviour can hinder their careers and affect their job satisfaction. Their need for constant reassurance and support can also strain relationships with colleagues and supervisors.

CLUSTER B IN DETAIL: THE ELEPHANT IN THE ROOM

Understanding Cluster B personality disorders, as categorized in the DSM-5, is important. Many people could avoid considerable suffering if they were more familiar with these disorders and knew how to manage interactions with those who have them. Cluster B includes Antisocial Personality Disorder, Borderline Personality Disorder, Histrionic Personality Disorder, and Narcissistic Personality Disorder. They share common features of impulsivity and erratic emotions but differ in specific characteristics.

Antisocial Personality Disorder (ASPD)

Antisocial Personality Disorder is characterized by a long-term pattern of disregard for, and violation of, the rights of others. This behaviour begins in childhood or early adolescence and continues into adulthood. Key traits of ASPD include deceitfulness, manipulation, selfishness, and lack of conscience.

Individuals with ASPD often behave aggressively towards people and animals, destroy property, and consistently violate laws and social norms. They habitually lie, use aliases, and con others, sometimes for personal gain, and sometimes without an obvious reason. Their actions are often impulsive, showing a purposeful disregard for consequences. They display irritability, aggressiveness, and a reckless indifference to their own safety or the safety of others. They also consistently fail to fulfil work, financial, and social obligations, often having no remorse for the harm they cause, instead blaming their victims and justifying their actions.

Research shows that ASPD affects approximately 0.2 to 3.3 per cent of the general population, but it is more common in certain groups. Among prison inmates, up to 50 to 80 per cent may have ASPD. In mental health institutions, the rate is also especially higher: around 15 to 25 per cent. The disorder is more common in people affected by adverse socioeconomic conditions, suggesting a complex interplay between ASPD, substance abuse and poverty.

Borderline Personality Disorder (BPD)

Borderline Personality Disorder involves instability in interpersonal relationships, self-image, and emotions, typically beginning in early adulthood and continuing into later life. People with BPD often go to great lengths to avoid real or imagined abandonment, leading to major changes in self-image, affect, perception, and behaviour.

People with BPD are extremely sensitive to their surroundings and may react with intense, inappropriate anger, even to brief separations or unavoidable changes in plans. Their relationships are often unstable and intense, with shifts between idealising and devaluing others. This instability also affects their self-image, which is often very unstable. 149

The diagnostic criteria for Borderline Personality Disorder include impulsivity in at least two self-damaging areas (e.g., excessive spending, risky sexual behaviour, substance abuse, reckless driving, binge eating). Additionally, repeated suicidal behaviour, gestures, or threats, and self-harming are common. Individuals with BPD often experience emotional instability, including rapid mood swings, chronic feelings of emptiness, inappropriate intense anger, and short-term stress-related paranoid thoughts or severe dissociative symptoms.

Estimates suggest that BPD affects 1.6 to 5.9 per cent of the general population. The disorder is more common in clinical settings, affecting about 10 per cent of outpatient mental health patients and up to 20 per cent of psychiatric inpatients.

Histrionic Personality Disorder (HPD)

Histrionic Personality Disorder is characterised by excessive emotionality and attention-seeking behaviour, beginning in early adulthood and occurring in various situations. People with HPD are uncomfortable or feel unappreciated when they are not the centre of attention. Often lively and dramatic, they tend to draw attention to themselves and may initially charm new acquaintances with their enthusiasm, apparent openness, and flirtatiousness. However, these qualities soon wear thin as individuals with HPD continually demand to be the centre of attention.

To stay in the spotlight, individuals with HPD may act inappropriately sexually seductive or provocative. They show rapidly shifting and shallow emotions, constantly using their physical appearance to draw attention to themselves and have a style of speech that is overly impressionistic and lacking in detail. Their emotional expression is theatrical and exaggerated. They are easily influenced by others or circumstances and view relationships as more intimate than they actually are.

Histrionic Personality Disorder affects about 2 per cent of the general population.

Narcissistic Personality Disorder (NPD)

Narcissistic Personality Disorder shares some similarities with Antisocial Personality Disorder but focuses on grandiosity and the need for admiration. Individuals with NPD have an inflated sense of their own importance, exaggerate their achievements and talents, and expect to be seen as superior without corresponding achievements. They fantasise about unlimited success, power, brilliance, beauty, or ideal love in their lives.

People with NPD believe they are special and unique and can only be understood by, or should associate with, other special or high-status people. They require excessive admiration, have a sense of entitlement, and expect favourable treatment or automatic compliance with their expectations. They exploit interpersonal relationships, taking advantage of others to achieve their own goals, and they lack empathy, being unwilling to recognize or identify with the feelings and needs of others. They often experience envy or believe others are envious of them and display arrogant behaviours or attitudes.

NPD affects up to 6.2 per cent of the general population, with higher rates observed in clinical settings.

Factors making individuals susceptible to victimisation by cluster B personality disorders:

Low self-esteem: People with low self-esteem may struggle to assert themselves or set boundaries, making them more likely to tolerate abusive behaviours from individuals with Cluster B personality disorders.

High empathy: Those with high empathy often try to understand and assist individuals with these disorders, sometimes at the expense of their own well-being. Their compassion can be taken advantage of by those who are manipulative.

Dependency: Individuals who heavily rely on others for emotional or financial support may be especially vulnerable. Their need for support could lead them to endure abusive behaviours to maintain the relationship.

History of trauma: People with a history of trauma, particularly childhood abuse or neglect, may be more prone to entering relationships with individuals who exhibit similar abusive behaviours. Past experiences can make them more tolerant of mistreatment.

Lack of social support: Those with weak social networks may find it challenging to leave abusive relationships. Isolation can worsen the impact of victimization, making it harder for individuals to seek help or recognize the abusive nature of the relationship.

Understanding these factors helps you recognize vulnerabilities and take steps to protect yourself from potential harm in relationships involving Cluster B personality disorders. Building self-awareness and establishing healthy boundaries are crucial for maintaining emotional well-being and navigating relationships effectively.

QUESTIONS FOR RELATIONSHIP EVALUATION

To better understand your relationships, consider these questions about yourself and the people you are close with:

Are they showing typical behaviour, or do they have a mental disorder?

It is important to recognize and distinguish between typical behaviour and symptoms of mental illness. Understanding mental health can improve your empathy and interactions. Additionally, this awareness can help you protect yourself from potential negative impacts.

Unfortunately, many people assume they can change others and cure their psychological disorders. The simple truth is, if you are with someone you want to change, then you are indeed with the wrong person. People change only when they choose to, and they do so through tangible, obvious steps. Often, there is a gap between what people say and what they do. Hence, it is crucial to focus on facts, current behaviour, track record and future prospects. Also, helping people with mental disorders is far more complex and challenging than it may initially appear.

Are they selfish, Machiavellian or narcissistic?

Identifying traits of selfishness, Machiavellianism, or narcissism can help you reach a better understanding of yourself and others, and manage interactions while setting healthy boundaries. These traits often lead to manipulative or self-centred behaviours that strain relationships. Recognizing these patterns allows you to implement strategies

such as clear communication and firm boundaries to protect your well-being, ensuring healthier, more balanced
interactions or terminating the relationship if necessary.
Research shows that addressing these traits early can prevent long-term negative impacts on mental health.

Are your relationships healthy or harmful?

Weighing up the health of your relationships involves assessing mutual respect, support and communication. Toxic relationships can harm your mental and emotional well-being,
leading to stress, anxiety and lower self-esteem. Recognize
these harmful dynamics early so you will know what steps
to take to protect yourself and seek healthier connections.

What do you need from every relationship?

Clarifying, assessing and reassessing your needs and what
you are willing to give in a relationship helps create balanced connections where both parties feel valued and
benefit fairly. This process ensures healthy give-and-take
dynamics. Discussing your contributions fosters mutual
understanding, openness, respect and growth. This re-
flection and dialogue support the development of strong,
healthy relationships that enhance the overall well-being
of both individuals involved.

Who are you in this relationship?

Understanding your identity and role within each relationship helps you stay authentic and avoid role conflicts,
leading to more stable and fulfilling connections.

Chapter 8.
The real solution

A man in rehab once asked me, 'What's the alternative to addiction? If I stop smoking crack, what should I do? You need to give us an alternative. What should I smoke?' This question highlights a common misconception that every void must be filled. It is like asking a doctor, 'If you remove my tumour, what will you replace it with? A better tumour?'

Some people argue that scientists mock pseudo-science without offering alternatives. The truth is, it's not the job of science to provide substitutes for every disproved myth. Science is about discovering the truth, not replacing every falsehood. Just as doctors remove an abscess to heal the body, scientists debunk pseudo-science to heal the mind. The goal is to eliminate harmful elements, not replace them with other delusions. More importantly, we aim for people to decide for themselves and live as free, independent individuals. Scientists don't want to become leaders or healers surrounded by flocks of followers.

That being said, science does offer information and data that you can use to improve your life.

Throughout this book I have tried to show how mental disorders can impact our life quality and how scientific thinking is beneficial and superior to easy mythical thinking. I have discussed how people are capable of making their own choices and decisions and that what we really need is information rather than advice, warnings, or gurus.

The final piece of the puzzle is finding solutions to improve your life. Here are some of the methods science offers us to preserve and improve our cognitive abilities.

A LIFE-LONG JOURNEY

Brain plasticity, also known as neuroplasticity, refers to the brain's incredible ability to reorganize itself by forming new neuron (brain cell) connections throughout a person's life. This remarkable adaptability plays a crucial role in learning, memory retention, and recovery following brain injuries. Experience is a major stimulant for the brain plasticity. Recent research highlights that brain plasticity is not limited to childhood; it continues throughout adulthood and into old age, allowing for lifelong learning and mental development. If we were to view the brain as the maestro and the other organs as the musicians, having a fully functioning maestro ensures the entire band plays in perfect harmony.

Childhood and adolescence

During childhood and adolescence, your brain undergoes major structural and functional changes. It strengthens useful connections and prunes away the ones you do not need, boosting overall efficiency. This period is like a golden window where your brain is in its prime for growth and learning. Studies show that enriched environments and stimulating activities during these formative years can greatly boost cognitive development and intelligence. Learning new skills is far easier during childhood, thanks to the remarkable plasticity of the young brain.

Learning a language is a perfect example. Young children naturally absorb new languages just by being exposed to them, picking up on the subtleties of pronunciation, grammar and vocabulary, often without instruction. Research shows that infants as young as six months can distinguish between different languages, a skill that narrows down as they grow older and focus on their native language. The ideal time for learning a second language is before the age of seven to nine, when children can achieve near-native fluency.

Children are not just good at languages – they are great at learning all kinds of new skills. They are naturally curious and less afraid to make mistakes, which makes them more likely to practise and thus improve their skills. This fearlessness is less common in adults, who often feel self-conscious about making errors. Jean Piaget, a renowned child psychologist, emphasized that children learn best through exploration and interaction with their environment, which includes experimenting with language and receiving feedback from others.

Whether learning to play a musical instrument or taking up a new sport, starting early taps into the brain's incredible ability to develop. Children who start young in music often see benefits in areas such as language, spatial reasoning and even maths.

This is not just about childhood, though. Early learning sets the stage for long-term cognitive benefits. For example, bilingual children often have better problem-solving skills and multitasking abilities compared to their single-language peers. Those early years are not just about immediate learning, but about building a foundation for lifelong intelligence and growth.

How to keep your brain sharp in adulthood

Even as adults, our brains are still capable of amazing growth. While not as rapid as in childhood, adult brains can still form new brain cells. So, how can we keep our brains active and healthy?

Dive into new skills or languages, or challenge yourself with complex mental tasks. Any mentally stimulating activity will do – the richer the better. These activities not only keep you busy but promote cognitive health and can even boost your intelligence. Research shows that keeping your mind engaged throughout life can help you avoid cognitive decline and keep you mentally sharp.

It is never too late to learn and grow. Your brain's plasticity is a lifelong asset, so take advantage of it!

Old age

Contrary to the outdated belief that the aging brain is unchangeable, recent findings show that the elderly brain retains significant plasticity. Older adults can still form new neural connections, and mental stimulation is key to preserving cognitive functions. Engaging in activities such as puzzles, reading, social interactions and continuous learning can help maintain and even boost cognitive abilities.

Physical exercise also plays a vital role in brain health. It increases blood flow to the brain and supports the growth of new brain cells. So, stay active, keep learning and enjoy social interactions to keep your mind sharp as you age.

Rewire your mind

Rewiring the mind involves forming new neural pathways and strengthening existing ones, a process facilitated by brain plasticity. Here is how you can do it:

Learning and education: Keep challenging your brain with new information and skills to form new neural connections.

Physical exercise: Regular physical activity supports brain health by causing new neurons to form and improves the health of your veins and arteries, which in turn supports cognitive functions.

Healthy diet: Nutrition plays a vital role in brain health. Diets rich in antioxidants, good fats, vitamins and minerals can support brain function and protect against cognitive decline.

Social engagement: Maintain strong social connections and engage in social activities.

Psychology provides factual information and data, offering reliable ways to distinguish between healthy individuals and those with mental health disorders. It investigates the causes and occurrence of these disorders and provides treatments for them. As the scientific study of human behaviour, psychology enables a better understanding of human actions and mental processes. It is a science based on objective, verifiable facts and theories that can be challenged and discredited. This foundation ensures that psychological findings are reliable and open to scrutiny, contributing to a more accurate and comprehensive understanding of the human psyche.

159

BIBLIOGRAPHY

Chapter 1. Introduction
Cleckley, Hervey (1941/2020). *The Mask of Sanity*. Digireads.com

Chapter 2 . How psychology helps you
Freud, Sigmund. (1900). *The Interpretation of Dreams*. Leipzig: Franz
    Deuticke.
Skinner, Burrhus F. (1953). *Science and Human Behavior*. NY: Macmillan.
Szasz, Thomas. (1961). *The Myth of Mental Illness*. NY: Hoeber-Harper.
American Psychiatric Association. (2013). *Diagnostic and Statistical
    Manual of Mental Disorders* (5th ed.). Arlington, VA: American
    Psychiatric Publishing.
Linehan, Marsha M. (1993). *Cognitive-Behavioral Treatment of Border-
    line Personality Disorder*. New York: Guilford Press.
Nolen-Hoeksema, Susan. (2000). The Role of Rumination in Depres-
    sive Disorders and Mixed Anxiety/Depressive Symptoms. *Journal
    of Abnormal Psychology, 109*(3), 504-511.
Mojtabai, Ramin, & Olfson, Mark. (2011). Diagnostic Validity of Psy-
    chiatric Medications Prescribed in Primary Care. *Psychiatric Ser-
    vices, 62*(12), 1458-1463.
Brady, Kathleen T., Sonya E. Back, & Shannon F. Coffey. (2000). Sub-
    stance abuse and posttraumatic stress disorder. *Journal of Clinical
    Psychiatry, 61*(12), 1-12.
Rush, John A., and others. (2006). Acute and longer-term outcomes
    in depressed outpatients requiring one or several treatment steps:
    A STAR*D report. *Journal of the American Medical Association,
    295*(17), 1985-1993.
Lurie, Stephen. (2019). Off-label prescribing in psychiatry: The impor-
    tance of clinical experience and emerging evidence. *Journal of Psy-
    chiatric Practice, 25*(4), 285-297.

Chapter 3. Cases from psychology
Perry, Bruce D., & Szalavitz, Maia. (2006). *The Boy Who Was Raised as
    a Dog: And Other Stories from a Child Psychiatrist's Notebook*. New
    York: Basic Books.
Chapter 4. Irrational beliefs and their cost
Wyatt, Petronella (2020). *Feminism Has Left Middle-Aged Women Like
    Me Single, Childless, and Depressed*. The Telegraph.
Bellieni, Carlo V., & Buonocore, Giuseppe. (2013). Abortion and Psy-
    chiatry. *Psychiatry and Clinical Neurosciences, 67*(4), 301-310.
Fergusson, David M., Horwood, L. John, & Boden, Joseph M. (2008).

Abortion and Mental Health Disorders: Evidence from a 30-Year Longitudinal Study. *British Journal of Psychiatry, 193*(6), 444-451.

Lamblin, Bianca. (1993). *Mémoires d'une Jeune Fille Dérangée*. Paris: Editions Balland.

Sowell, Thomas. (1994). *Race and Culture: A World View*. Basic Books.

Sowell, Thomas. (2005). *Black Rednecks and White Liberals*. Encounter Books.

Pew Research Center. (2016). *On Views of Race and Inequality, Blacks and Whites Are Worlds Apart*.

NHS Digital (2019). *ADHD: Service and Statistics*.

Royal College of Psychiatrists (2018). *Position Statement on Antidepressants and Depression*.

Hirschfeld, Robert M.A., and others. (2003). Perceptions and impact of bipolar disorder: how far have we really come? *Bipolar Disorders*.

Parker, Gordon, and others. (2014). Misdiagnosis of Depression in the Community: Issues and Solutions. *Australian & New Zealand Journal of Psychiatry*.

Centers for Disease Control and Prevention (CDC). (2016). *Attention-Deficit/Hyperactivity Disorder (ADHD): Data & Statistics*.

Mojtabai, Ramin, & Olfson, Mark. (2011). National Trends in the Prevalence and Treatment of Depression in the United States. *JAMA*.

NIMH statistics on mental health prevalence: National Institute of Mental Health (NIMH) online.

World Health Organization. (2019). *Mental health in the workplace*.

Carter, Robert T., and others. (2013). Racial discrimination and PTSD: The mediating role of racial identity. *Journal of Trauma & Dissociation*.

Health and Safety Executive (HSE). (2020). Work-related Stress, Anxiety or Depression Statistics.

Centers for Disease Control and Prevention (CDC). (2016). *2016 National Survey of Children's Health*.

Quote on Epicurus from: Rist, John M. (1980). Epicurus on friendship. *Classical Philology, 75*, 121–129.

Additional reading:

Festinger, Leon. (1957). *A Theory of Cognitive Dissonance*. Stanford University Press.

Beck, Aaron T. (1976). *Cognitive Therapy and the Emotional Disorders*. International Universities Press.

Chapter 5. Self-help books between science and opium

Freud, Sigmund. (1930). *Civilization and Its Discontents*. Leipzig: Internationaler Psychoanalytischer Verlag.

Robbins, Tony. (1991/2001). *Awaken the Giant Within: How to Take Immediate Control of Your Mental, Emotional, Physical and Financial Destiny!*

Geller, Uri. (1975). *My Story: The Bendest of the Spoon-Benders*. Henry Holt & Company.

Sincero, Jen. (2013). *You Are a Badass: How to Stop Doubting Your Greatness and Start Living an Awesome Life*. Philadelphia: Running Press.

Byrne, Rhonda. (2006). *The Secret*. New York: Atria Books.

Clear, James. (2018). *Atomic Habits: An Easy & Proven Way to Build Good Habits & Break Bad Ones*. New York: Avery.

Manson, Mark. (2016). *The Subtle Art of Not Giving a F*ck: A Counterintuitive Approach to Living a Good Life*. New York: HarperOne.

BBC Sport, 2012. *British Cycling and Lottery Funding: The impact of lottery funding on British sport*.

Draper, Kevin. *The making of Team Sky: Inside the world's best cycling team*. Sky Sports, 2019.

Ingle, Sean. *How Team Sky broke the cycling mould*. BBC Sport, 2019.

Richardson, Simon. (2008). *From paupers to kings: The lottery-funded revolution*. Cycling Weekly.

Chapter 6. Understanding yourself

Goffman, Erving. (1959). *The Presentation of Self in Everyday Life*. Anchor Books.

Tajfel, Henri, & Turner, John C. (1979). *An integrative theory of intergroup conflict*. In W. G. Austin & S. Worchel (Eds.), *The Social Psychology of Intergroup Relations* (pp. 33-47). Brooks/Cole Publishing.

Coid, Jeremy, and others. (2006). Prevalence and correlates of personality disorder in Great Britain. *British Journal of Psychiatry, 188*(5), 423-431.

Fazel, Seena, & Danesh, John. (2002). Serious mental disorder in 23,000 prisoners: A systematic review of 62 surveys. *The Lancet, 359*(9306), 545-550.

Lynam, Donald R., & Miller, Joshua D. (2015). Psychopathy from a basic trait perspective: The utility of a five-factor model approach. *Journal of Personality, 83*(6), 660-674.

Lenzenweger, Mark F., and others. (2007). DSM-IV personality disorders in the National Comorbidity Survey Replication. *Biological Psychiatry, 62*(6), 553-564.

Millon, Theodore, & Davis, Roger D. (1996). *Disorders of Personality: DSM-IV and Beyond*. Wiley.

Torgersen, Svenn, Kringlen, Einar, & Cramer, Victoria. (2001). The prevalence of personality disorders in a community sample. *Archives of General Psychiatry, 58*(6), 590-596

Millon, Theodore, & Davis, Roger D. (1996). Disorders of Personality: DSM-IV and Beyond. Wiley.

Stinson, Frederick S., and others. (2008). Prevalence, correlates, disability, and comorbidity of DSM-IV narcissistic personality disorder: Results from the Wave 2 National Epidemiologic Survey on Alcohol and Related Conditions. *Journal of Clinical Psychiatry, 69*(7).

Myers, Lisa, & Zeigler-Hill, Virgil. (2012). The influence of low self-esteem on the interpersonal relationships of individuals with Cluster B personality disorders. *Journal of Personality Disorders, 26*(4), 423-435.

Cohen, Sheldon, & Wills, Thomas A. (1985). Stress, social support, and the buffering hypothesis. *Psychological Bulletin, 98*(2), 310-357.

Additional reading:

Locke, Edwin A., & Latham, Gary P. (2002). Building a Practically Useful Theory of Goal Setting and Task Motivation: A 35-Year Odyssey. *American Psychologist, 57*(9), 705-717.

Snyder, Charles R. (2002). Hope Theory: Rainbows in the Mind. *Psychological Inquiry, 13*(4), 249-275.

Chapter 7. Understanding others

McCrae, Robert R., & Costa, Paul T. (2008). *The Five-Factor Model of Personality*. Guilford Press.

Costa, Paul T., & McCrae, Robert R. (1992). Revised NEO Personality Inventory (NEO-PI-R) and NEO Five-Factor Inventory (NEO-FFI) professional manual. Odessa, FL: *Psychological Assessment Resources*.

American Psychiatric Association. (2013). *Diagnostic and Statistical Manual of Mental Disorders* (5th ed.). Arlington, VA: American Psychiatric Publishing.

Chapter 8. The real solution

Deary, Ian J. (2012). Intelligence. *Annual Review of Psychology, 63*, 453-482.

Kuhl, Patricia K. (2010). Brain mechanisms in early language acquisition. *Neuron, 67*(5), 713-727.

Penfield, Wilder, & Roberts, Lamar. (1959). *Speech and Brain Mechanisms*. Princeton, NJ: Princeton University Press.

Johnson, Jeffrey S., & Newport, Elissa L. (1989). Critical period effects in second language learning: The influence of maturational state on the acquisition of English as a second language. *Cognitive Psychology, 21*(1), 60-99.

Penhune, Virginia B. (2011). Sensitive periods in human development: Evidence from musical training. *Cortex, 47*(9), 1126-1137.

Bialystok, Ellen. (2009). Bilingualism: The good, the bad, and the indifferent. *Bilingualism: Language and Cognition, 12*(1), 3-11.

Deary, Ian J., Whalley, Lawrence J., & Starr, John M. (2009). *A Lifetime of Intelligence: Follow-up Studies of the Scottish Mental Surveys of 1932 and 1947*. Washington, DC: American Psychological Association.